# Ministry and Community

## Recognizing, Healing, and Preventing Ministry Impairment

*Len Sperry*

*A Liturgical Press Book*

THE LITURGICAL PRESS
Collegeville, Minnesota

Cover design by David Manahan, O.S.B.

The author is grateful to The Jesuit Educational Center for Human Development, Silver Spring, Maryland, for permission to include in this book articles that he has published in the journal *Human Development* and which have been revised.

| 1 | 2 | 3 | 4 | 5 | 6 | 7 | 8 |
| --- | --- | --- | --- | --- | --- | --- | --- |

**Library of Congress Cataloging-in-Publication Data**

Sperry, Len.
    Ministry and community : recognizing, healing, and preventing ministry impairment / Len Sperry.
        p.    cm.
    Includes bibliographical references and index.
    ISBN 0-8146-2723-4 (alk. paper)
    1. Clergy—Mental health.   2. Personality disorders—Religious aspects—Christianity.   3. Organizational behavior—Religious aspects—Christianity.   4. Church work—Psychology.   I. Title.
BV4398.S64   2000
253'.2—dc21                          99-042557
                                            CIP

# MINISTRY AND COMMUNITY

# Contents

# Preface

The mass media is increasingly reporting instances of brokenness and impairment in ministry which involve sexual acting out, fraudulent behavior, drug abuse, and other behavior unbecoming ministry personnel. Dioceses, judiciaries, and religious organizations are becoming wearied by negative publicity, lawsuits, and claims for compensatory and punitive damages. Many, including the media, assume that these troublesome deeds can be attributed entirely to the vulnerabilities and psychopathology of a small number of individual ministers. In actuality, the infrastructure and the culture of the church community can foster and reinforce much of this pathological or unbecoming behavior. For instance, by accepting certain candidates for ministry training and providing a milieu that reinforces certain attitudes and behavior, the Church may unwittingly collude in the development and expression of certain behaviors and pathologies.

For many, ministry evokes a sense of mystery, care and concern, idealism and even heroic courage. Images like "wounded healers" are often evoked and suggest that ministers gain much of their power to comfort and support those in pain and turmoil by working through and transcending their own woundedness. While this image is valid, it is nevertheless true that ministers can also be "wounding healers," and that the church community can unwittingly "wound" ministers and others and reinforce their wounding behaviors. For ministry to be truly effective and a source of holiness and wholeness, the personality and organizational dynamics underlying, and in many cases causing such impairment and woundedness need first to be carefully identified and then to be realistically modified.

This book examines the personality dynamics of these vulnerable ministers as well as the organizational dynamics that foster various kinds of pathology and acting-out behaviors. It looks at the dynamics underlying and supporting narcissistic behavior, sexual-abusing behavior, psychopathic behavior, borderline behavior, depressive behavior, obsessive-compulsive behavior, manic-depressive behavior, and passive-aggressive behavior in ministry personnel. It then describes a number of effective strategies that can modify these individual and organizational dynamics.

While it may be fashionable to criticize the structure, culture or leadership of the church community as dysfunctional or toxic, this is not the purpose or intention of this book. Rather than affix blame on ministers or the Church, this book offers a series of observations on some pressing concerns faced by the Church and then provides several suggestions for addressing these concerns. This book intends to offer a measure of hopefulness about the prospects for professional ministry in the evolving community called Church. These suggestions include specific criterion for determining fitness for ministry, guidelines for realistically appraising ministry performance, and specific indications and contraindications for psychotherapy and other psychiatric interventions.

Currently, there is relatively little written about ministry from the perspective of personality dynamics and organizational dynamics. This is the first book to describe and integrate both sets of dynamics. My work as a practicing clinical psychiatrist who specializes in treating ministry personnel and consulting to Church communities—such as religious Orders, parishes, professional religious organizations, and dioceses—has given me experience with and insight into the challenges facing ministries and Church communities today. This book is my effort to share this experience and insights.

The book should have some interest for those taking courses in the broad area of pastoral ministry, pastoral counseling and psychotherapy, as well as religion and personality, and psychotherapy and religion/spirituality. Hopefully, it will be of value to religious leaders and formation staff who are charged with screening ministry candidates and preparing them for various ministries. Professional clinicians who assess, evaluate and treat ministry candidates and ministry personnel may find it useful in their work. Finally, I hope that this book can be of some value to those who minister to others as well as to those to whom they minister.

Len Sperry, M.D., Ph.D.

# Acknowledgments

Although writing a book such as this is largely a solitary activity, it is also a community effort of sorts. There are a number of individuals who have given generously of their time and expertise to review and critique earlier versions of this manuscript. In particular, I want to mention James Gill, S.J., M.D., editor-in-chief, and Linda Amadeo, executive editor, of *Human Development* who have encouraged me to turn parts of this manuscript that were published as articles in *Human Development* into a book. Most Reverend Rembert Weakland, O.S.B., D.D., Archbishop of Milwaukee, and Most Reverend Richard Sklba, Ph.D., auxiliary bishop of Milwaukee, also offered considerable encouragement as this project was in process. I especially want to express my gratitude to Bishop Sklba for his helpful theological clarifications on moral indicators of fitness for ministry. These clarifications are described throughout the book, particularly in the Appendix. Furthermore, my appreciation to Elizabeth Piasecki, Psy.D., Director of Project Benjamin of the Archdiocese of Milwaukee, Rev. Louis Lussier, M.D., Ph.D., O.S.Cam., and the Rev. Matthew Linn, S.J., for their input on ministry fitness in clerical formation programs. Finally, my thanks to Jeremy Langford of Sheed & Ward for his editorial critique, and to Mark Twomey, managing editor, and Colleen Stiller, production manager, at The Liturgical Press for making this book a reality.

# 1

## Ministry and Community Today: An Overview

There is a sense of mystery surrounding Christian ministry, as well for those individuals who are called to become and function as ministers. Psychological models can be incredibly valuable in understanding ministry, particularly when a model provides a dual perspective involving both personality dynamics and organizational dynamics. But even such a dual perspective cannot provide a complete understanding, since additional pastoral, theological, and historical perspectives should also be considered. This book focuses on personality and organizational dynamics, and so provides a useful, but necessarily limited, perspective through which to capture some sense of the mystery that surrounds ministry. Though limited, this dual perspective provides a powerful and penetrating view. It is like a lighthouse beacon that can guide ships in the night, but it cannot illuminate the skies as the sun does. While this dual lens provides a broader perspective than a single lens that simply views only personality dynamics or only organizational dynamics, nevertheless, this dual lens provides a necessary but not sufficient understanding of personal and contextual issues in ministry settings.

Acknowledging this limitation is necessary, particularly in an age when psychological explanations for complex realities are often uncritically reified and accepted. This chapter introduces the reader to the problem of and issues of impairment and the topics of personality dynamics and organizational dynamics. A basic premise of the book is that organizational dynamics can trigger and reinforce the personality dynamics of ministers who become impaired.

Subsequent chapters describe the dynamics of eight impaired personality patterns, including their characteristic interpersonal and religious and spiritual attitudes and behaviors. How and why these particular patterns evolve and are reinforced by organizational dynamics will also be discussed. In addition, each chapter describes a number of interventions for modifying these personality dynamics and organizational dynamics. But, first some preliminary comments about distress and impairment in ministry.

## Impairment in Ministry

Impairment, which is also referred to as distress and dysfunction, needs to be distinguished from normal and distressed functioning. A distressed minister is an active functioning member of a pastoral team, diocese, or religious community who cannot consistently function well in his or her ministry due to occasional internal and external stressors. On the other hand, an impaired minister is unable to function in ministry because of a debilitating medical condition or a dysfunctional pattern of behavior that reflects a lack of "fit" or negative interaction between a predisposed minister and his or her assignment in a given diocese or province (Sperry, 1993). While fears and anxiety, fluctuating moods, burnout symptoms, job dissatisfaction, and doubts about career and vocation are experienced by distressed ministers, manic depressive illness, major depressive disorder, psychosis, alcoholism or drug addiction, or a sexual disorder are conditions experienced by impaired ministers.

## Determinants of Impairment

For the most part ministry impairment is understood and explained as a personal deficit or defect in the individual minister. Many believe that ministers prone to impairment are psychologically immature or have inadequate coping skills or may have been abused as children or have family histories of mental disorders, and so on. It should not be surprising that many religious superiors and those in episcopal governance subscribe to the "deficit-defect" explanation. However, there are others who believe that distress and impairment are as much a function of organizational structure, culture, leadership style, and the individual minister's theology of ministry as they are of the individual's physical and psychological vulnerabilities and coping skills, and specific stressors associated with the individual's ministry.

According to this view, impairment can be determined and predictive by the degree of "fit" among the dimensions of minister, organization, vocation, and ministry assignment.

## Minister

The minister dimension refers to the individual minister's personality dynamics and self-esteem, health status, as well as the impact of heredity, early childhood, and family influences. It also refers to the individual's health beliefs and behaviors, such as weight, diet, sleep, and exercise habits and coping skills.

## Organization

Organization refers to the organization's dynamics, particularly its structure, norms, and culture. These include the degree of role clarity or ambiguity, its system of rewards, sanctions, and control, as well as organizational culture. This culture will reflect a particular image of God as well as beliefs about the goals and purposes of ministry.

## Vocation

Vocation refers to the way the minister views professional roles, responsibilities, and expectations based on his or her call to ministry and theology of ministry.

## Ministry Assignment

Ministry assignment refers to the specific stressors, job demands, and expectations of one's ministry as well as the support system and benefits of a particular ministry. It includes the minister's perceived sense of control and decision making regarding job demands, and the degree of job satisfaction. A good fit can "buffer" even a minister with some coping skill deficits, while a poor fit could conceivably distress or otherwise impair a high-functioning individual (Sperry, 1991).

**Personality Dynamics**

Personality may be thought of as the stable and enduring patterns that influence an individual's perceptions, thoughts, feelings, and actions. Such patterns define us as the unique individuals we are. Those patterns that are healthy and adaptive are designated as personality styles. Those that are overly rigid, maladaptive, and affect others negatively are called personality disorders. To keep matters in perspective, the distinction between a trait and a personality disorder needs to be made. Any person can manifest one or more of the traits or features of any of the personality styles without possessing the extremely rigid, compulsive, and maladaptive pattern of that style. It might be useful to think of personality patterns, both styles and disorders, in terms of a bell curve as in Figure 1.

On the bell curve, personality style can be visualized by the ascending or upward curve, while the personality disorder can be designated by the declining, downward curve.

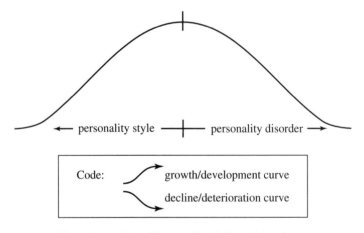

*Figure 1: The Relationship of Personality Style to Disorder*

Is a personality disorder the same as a neurosis, i.e., an emotional disorder or disturbance? Actually, there are two types of neurosis: psychoneurosis and character neurosis. Intense anxiety, pain, and suffering are experienced by those with a psychoneurosis. Persons with a character neurosis impose pain, discomfort, and suffering on others. Character neurosis is synonymous with personality disorder.

In this discussion, personality disorders are considered pathological extensions of the personality patterns. That is to say that the personality disorders emerge out of personality patterns as a result of a complex interaction of early life experiences, parenting styles, environmental stressors, maladaptive learning, and even biological predisposition.

## *Personality Styles vs. Personality Disorders*

Personality patterns are of two types: styles and disorders. The disordered pattern, originally called the character neurosis, is rigid and maladaptive and negatively impacts others. That is, others experience varying degrees of anger and suffering as a result of relating to individuals with disordered personalities. Most individuals have a mix of two or more personality patterns that makes them unique. It is rare for a minister to have a pure personality type, for example, only narcissistic personality dynamics or only passive-aggressive personality dynamics. For didactic purposes, however, each subsequent chapter will describe pure types.

Where an individual minister resides on the continuum between personality styles and personality disorders is, in part, a function of early-life experiences, but is largely a matter of day-to-day decisions. Just as virtues and vices are outcomes of a lifetime of positive or negative habits and disciplines which are related to moment-to-moment choices involving moral actions, so too is one's personality. The biblical correlate of the personality disorder would be a "hardened heart," while a healthy personality would correspond to a "heart of flesh."

The more rigid and disordered ministers are, the more they adopt rigid conceptual categories and ideologies and "need" simple answers to complex problems and issues. Not surprisingly, they adopt rigid behavior patterns, particularly compulsive behaviors. Fortunately, psychotherapy and spiritual growth can transform these disordered patterns into healthier styles, at least in some instances.

Readers may recognize aspects of themselves in the descriptions of the various personalities described in chapters 2 through 9. For some, the temptation will be to discount or devalue this information because of preconceived ideas (e.g., "narcissism is always bad," "I've never been passive-aggressive") or to wish that the personality pattern were described in "safer," more everyday language, because of some fear of being thought of as mentally unstable. It is suggested that the reader keep in mind the concept of the continuum in reading about each personality style and guard against the temptation to diagnose self or others.

*Treatability of Ministry Impairment*

To what extent is change possible in a personality-disordered minister? This is, indeed, a complex question. Nevertheless, based on Stone's (1993) research it is possible to establish a "treatability index" for the various disorders of personality. By treatability is meant the likelihood that change via traditional psychotherapy or other change strategies will occur. Based on this index, the depressive and obsessive-compulsive personalities would be rated as highly treatable; borderline, manic-depressive, and narcissistic personalities would be rated as moderately treatable; and psychopathic, sexual-abusing and passive-aggressive personalities would be rated as minimally treatable.

Today, passive-aggressive behavior is rather common in ministry. But while it is present in some ministry settings, it is virtually absent in others. Why is this? The reason is that religious organizations with certain kinds of cultures or who are at a particular stage of organizational development tend to foster and reinforce passive-aggressivity. Referring to an organization's culture and developmental stage permits a transition to the topic of organizational dynamics.

## Organizational Dynamics

Like other professions and occupations, ministry takes place in an organizational context. Even though a minister may work only one-on-one with parishioners, spiritual directees, or diocesan personnel, that ministry is not simply an interpersonal, dyadic relationship. That ministry is influenced by the structures and culture of the institution or organization that sponsors and supports it. Ministry behavior is not simply then a function of the minister's personality dynamics; it is also a function of organizational dynamics.

Just as it is valuable to understand personality dynamics, it is essential to have a working knowledge of organizational dynamics to understand and change ministry personnel. It is surprising to many to learn that efforts to change a minister's personality dynamics with individual psychotherapy are often insufficient to effect permanent change because of the impact of these organizational dynamics. In other words, to really understand behavior in ministry settings it is essential to know about both personality and organizational dynamics.

A relatively simple way of understanding organizational dynamics is to think of an organization as a set of five overlapping, concentric circles representing the organization's subsystems of structure, culture, strategy, leaders, and members within a larger circle representing the organization's external environment. In addition, every organization has a developmental stage that situates these other six dimensions in terms of the organization's cycle of growth or decline (Sperry, 1996). Each of these will be briefly described.

**Structure** refers to mechanisms that aid an organization to achieve its intended task and goals. The task is divided into smaller person-sized jobs or roles and grouped and clustered into larger sets such as ministry teams, diocesan or provincialate staff, and so on. It specifies the reporting relationship of all roles, their span of control and scope of authority, and their location in a hierarchy of roles, called an organizational chart. An organization's structural system specifies the ways in which the person within a role performs. It is the means of measuring job performance, which is called a "performance appraisal system." Roles are expectations which prescribe the boundaries of acceptable behavior for a particular job and the individual or individuals holding that job. Norms, on the other hand, define group behavior. Norms are shared group expectations about what constitutes appropriate behavior.

**Culture** refers to the constellation of shared experiences, beliefs, assumptions, stories, customs, and actions that characterize an organization. The major determinants of culture are the values held by leaders of that organization, the history of the organization, and the current leader's vision of the organization. In a religious Order, often the founder's vision and the community's charism may still significantly influence the current culture. These translate into culture through the shared experiences, memories, stories, and actions of its members. The corporate culture provides a guide to action for new situations and for new members. Culture is to the organization what personality and temperament are to the individual. Thus, culture defines an organization's identity to both those inside and outside the organization. The culture of a corporation may be difficult to describe in words, but everyone senses it. It gives an organization its unique "flavor" and is "the way we do things around here." It subtly controls the behavior of its members. Accordingly, management can influence its members by effectively managing the organization's culture.

The **leader** subsystem involves both the leadership and management functions of an organization. Leadership refers to a process of influence whereby a leader persuades, enables, or empowers others to pursue and achieve the intended goals of the organization. Leadership and management were terms that are sometimes used synonymously. There are at least three ways of conceptualizing the leadership process. One way is to assume that effective leaders have the flexibility to shift their style from being "boss-centered," called the autocratic style, to "employee-centered," called the participative style to accommodate the needs of specific situations. A second way is to think of leadership as combining two styles simultaneously, but in different proportions. One style is task-centered, the other being employee or person-centered. A third way of thinking about leadership considers three factors. Called "situational leadership" the best form of leadership is based on situational needs: the personal characteristics of the leaders, the nature of the organization, and worker characteristics.

The **member** subsystem involves the way employees relate to each other, their leaders, and the organization's mission and specific goals. Also called "followership" style, this subsystem is an important key to a leader's and the organization's success. Research shows that members of an organization have a preference for either the autocratic, democratic, or participative leadership style. Workers function best with leadership that corresponds with their followership style. For example, a subordinate with an affinity for the autocratic approach will respond favorably to the autocratic leadership style. The lack of match between leadership and followership styles probably accounts for conflict, stress, decreased worker productivity and performance.

**Strategy** refers to the organization's overall plan or course of action for achieving its identified goals. Corporate strategy is based on the organization's vision and mission statements. The vision statement answers the question: "What can the organization become, and why?" while the mission statement answers the "What business are we in, and who is our customer?" question. Strategy answers the "How do we do it?" question.

The environment supra-system refers to those factors outside an organizational system that influence it and interact with it. The environment includes economic, legal, political, and sociocultural factors. For a parish this might mean the larger community's level of employment, level of education, the bishop's liberal or conservative leanings, and diocesan resources to support the parish's mission.

**Developmental stage** refers to the organization's stage of development and is somewhat akin to an individual's stage of development (for example, childhood, adolescence, early adulthood, middle age, old age). Organizations proceed through various stages from beginning, expansion, professionalization, consolidation, and early and late bureaucratization. Figure 2 depicts these stages of growth and decline on a bell curve (cf. Sperry, 1989, 1996, for a detailed description of the stages).

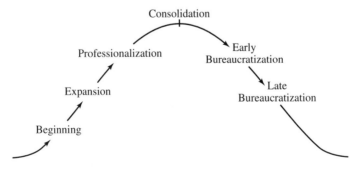

*Figure 2: Developmental Stages of an Organization*

It should be noted that communities that are in the stage of early or late bureaucratization are most likely to foster and reinforce passive-aggressive behavior and overdependency. Finally, the organizational dimensions of structure, culture, and leadership will be highlighted in the community-focused or organizational change activities suggested in subsequent chapters.

## Concluding Note

This chapter has introduced the dimensions of personality dynamics and organizational dynamics as they related to ministry. From this dual perspective lens it is possible to conceptualize and change or modify impairment in ministers as well as in those dysfunctional ministry settings that foster and reinforce this impairment. Subsequent chapters will focus on eight behavior patterns or personality disorders commonly seen in ministry settings. Occasionally, referral for individual psychotherapy is sufficient to effect major change in a minister's behavior. However, most often individual psychotherapy and/or medication is insufficient. The reason for this is that community and organizational dynamics compound personality dynamics. Unless and until both sets of dynamics are addressed, the problem behavior is likely to continue and even intensify.

## References

Len Sperry, *Corporate Therapy and Consulting*. New York: Brunner/Mazel, 1996.

Len Sperry, "Determinants of a Minister's Well-Being," *Human Development* 12, no. 2 (1991) 21–26.

Len Sperry, "The Development of Organizations," *Human Development* 10, no. 2 (Summer 1989) 26–31.

Len Sperry, *Handbook of Diagnosis and Treatment of the DSM-IV Personality Disorders*. New York: Brunner/Mazel, 1995.

Len Sperry, *Psychiatric Consultation in the Workplace*. Washington, D.C.: American Psychiatric Press, 1993.

Michael Stone, *Abnormalities of Personality: Within and Beyond the Realm of Treatment*. New York: Norton, 1993.

# 2

## Narcissistic Behavior in Ministry

Trouble had been brewing for some time at All Saints Church but had recently erupted in this otherwise large, quiet suburban parish. Composed of a majority of retirees and young professional families, as well as a sizeable group of undergraduate and graduate students from a nearby private university, the parish had been relatively trouble-free since it was established.

A civil suit brought against the parish and the diocese by disgruntled parishioners had unleashed a torrent of sentiment within the parish to replace the liturgy director, the parish council, and the pastor. The suit alleged that the liturgy director had engaged in sexual impropriety with young women in the parish, and that while the pastor and parish council had been apprised of the matter they had failed to respond appropriately and in a timely fashion. The liturgy director was married, childless, in his late forties, and had been employed by the parish for four years. He had been hired after an exhaustive search to find someone with his credentials: a graduate degree in liturgy and successful experience with a large diverse parish. During his first few months at All Saints, his charm and wit had won over many skeptics, particularly among the older parishioners, who were not eager to replace traditional liturgies and devotions with the new. In a short time, he succeeded in commanding a sizable, loyal following. Nevertheless, his flamboyant manner led some to complain to the diocese and others to leave for a more compatible parish community. A subsequent diocesan report concluded that while the parish's liturgical and paraliturgical services were within liturgical guidelines the services were more like performances than occasions of worship.

The pastor had and continued to support the liturgy director through these times. On the surface, matters seemed to have settled down in the second and third years in the job. While he had always dressed impeccably in his third year, he became noticeably preoccupied with his appearance and signs of aging. He returned from an extended vacation with a new look: a face lift and hair transplant. Before he had arrived at All Saints, the liturgy committee had consisted of a number of mature men and women appointed by the previous pastor. Shortly thereafter, the committee composition changed dramatically to include young, attractive professional women who became extremely loyal to its new director. When rumors surfaced that the new pastor had placed some limitations on the director because of the complaints of impropriety and scandal, the liturgy committee members defended the director and turned on the pastor and parish council.

The individual just described exhibits narcissistic behavior and might even be called a narcissistic minister. He is also an individual who clearly meets the diagnostic criteria for narcissistic personality disorder. The reality is that individuals with a narcissistic pattern are attracted to ministries, particularly high visibility ministries and positions of leadership. Furthermore, narcissistic ministers are becoming increasingly common in religious organizations, including parishes, religious communities of men and women, and in diocesan and other ecclesial offices. Unfortunately, narcissistic ministers create an incredible amount of havoc in their ministry assignments. Previously, I briefly profiled this personality as one of six most common "neurotic personalities in religious settings" (Sperry, 1991).

Not all narcissistic ministers are the same, just as not all narcissistic politicians or executives are the same. Although much has been published about narcissistic psychopathology, relatively little has differentiated its variants or types, and none has described these types in religious settings. Accordingly, this chapter describes three variants, from clearly pathological to relatively healthy, of this personality among ministry personnel. Before focusing on these variants, it is helpful to describe the basic narcissistic dynamics common to all three.

## Dynamics of the Narcissistic Personality

Narcissistic ministers are typically heralded as individuals possessing great potential. Consequently, great things are expected of them, yet seldom is their full potential realized. While some of these individuals can be extremely effective ministers, eventually, and inevitably, problems arise. For one, their unceasing need for admiration and the exploitative nature of their relationships are becoming irritating. As time goes by their ministerial presence seems less than genuine, having a gamy quality to it. In their striving for success they easily and readily manipulate others. Typically, it is significant stressors such as the onset of physical aging, career setbacks, and the increasing experience of the emptiness in their relationships that precipitates crises in their lives and trouble in their ministries.

Narcissists believe they must rely on themselves rather than on others for the gratification of their needs. They live with the conviction that it is unsafe to depend on anyone's love or loyalty. Instead, they pretend to be self-sufficient. But, in the depths of their being they experience a sense of deprivation and emptiness. To cope with these feelings and assuage their insecurity, narcissistic individuals become preoccupied with establishing their power, appearance, status, prestige, and superiority. At the same time, they expect others to recognize their entitlement and specialness, and meet their needs. What is particularly striking is their interpersonal exploitativeness. Narcissistic individuals live under the illusion that they are entitled to be served, that their own desires take precedence over those of others, and that they deserve special consideration in life.

It must be emphasized, however, that these characteristics occur with different degrees of intensity. A certain dose of narcissism is necessary to function effectively. All individuals exhibit some narcissistic behavior. Among individuals who possess only modest narcissistic tendencies are those who are very talented and capable of making great contributions to society. However, those who gravitate toward the pathological extreme give narcissism its pejorative reputation.

Narcissistic ministers occupy different positions on a spectrum ranging from healthy narcissism to pathological narcissism. Three types of variants of narcissism in ministers will be described. These descriptions have been adapted from the types of narcissism among executives and leaders developed by Kets de Vries (1989), an organization psychologist. For him the factors that distinguish between health and dysfunction are intrapsychic and interpersonal dynamics. The DSM-IV makes the distinction in behavioral terms, listing nine criteria: a grandiose sense of self-importance or uniqueness; a preoccupation with fantasies of unlimited success, power, brilliance, beauty or ideal love; a sense of specialness; a need for excessive admiration from others; interpersonal exploitativeness; entitlement; arrogance and haughtiness; being envious of others; and a lack of empathy. Meeting five or more of these criteria suggests the diagnosis of narcissistic personality disorder, while fewer than five suggest narcissistic traits. The enneagram provides another means of characterizing the narcissistic personality. The "three," characterized by striving for success and achievement, best reflects this personality. In enneagram parlance, an "unredeemed" three would probably correlate with the first and second types described below, while the "redeemed" three would probably correlate with the third type. These types are: reactive narcissism, self-deceptive narcissism, and constructive narcissism.

*Reactive Narcissism*

Ministers exhibiting reactive narcissism clearly meet diagnostic criteria for the narcissistic personality disorder but also exhibit features of other personality disorders such as the sadistic, paranoid, and antisocial or sociopathic personality. While they appear to be charming and engaging, they can just as easily be cold, calculating, and ruthless. According to Kets de Vries, these individuals suffer from severe developmental deficits. Normal development involves two important spheres of the self. The first is the tendency to obtain reassurance through recognition, praise, and admiration which is called "mirroring," referred to as the "grandiose self," while the second is the tendency to feel

powerful through identification and idealization of another—
referred to as the "idealized parental image." Both of these are
poorly integrated in the reactive narcissist.

Phase-appropriate development in the early years did not occur
in reactive narcissists. Frustrating experiences were poorly handled.
As children, they acquired instead a defective, poorly integrated
sense of identity and subsequently were unable to maintain a stable
sense of self-esteem and a cohesive sense of self. To cope with such
feelings, these individuals created for themselves a self-view of
specialness, which was a compensation against a constant feeling
of never having been loved by their parents. The internal world of
these narcissistic ministers was very likely populated by traumatic
and malevolent images, for which they cannot forget and continually fail to master but to which they continually react.

Creating the illusion of uniqueness is one method of coping or
mastery, but a brittle one. This inner fragility impacts their dealings
with the external environment. Any discrepancies between capacities and wants are likely to accentuate anxiety and impair reality
testing. As such these individuals tend to distort outside events to
manage anxiety and to prevent a sense of loss and disappointment.
Examples of such individuals are the Hitlers, Kohmenis, and others
whom Scott Peck, M.D., calls "people of the lie," i.e., individuals
whose actions appear to reflect a sense of evilness, and Otto Kern-
berg, M.D., diagnoses as "malignant narcissists."

Reactive narcissists who are in major positions of religious
leadership can cause considerable trouble. They tend to surround
themselves with followers who are sycophants. They exhibit little or
no concern about hurting others in pursuit of their own interests, and
readily devalue others to underscore their own superiority. Because
of significant empathic deficit in their personality structure, they
have little awareness or appreciation for other's needs and feelings.
Projects are undertaken on a grand scale but are often doomed to
failure because of lack of judgment and an absence of reality testing.
Predictably, when things go wrong, they blame others.

## Self-Deceptive Narcissism

The second type of narcissistic minister also meets the criteria
for the narcissistic personality disorder, but does not exhibit the ex-

tremes of cruelty and paranoia as the reactive narcissist. The self-deceptive narcissist experiences a rather different pattern of early childhood development. During early development these ministers were probably overstimulated or overburdened. One or both parents led them to believe that they were completely lovable and perfect, regardless of their actions and in spite of reality. Such children become the proxies of their parents, entrusted with a mission to fulfill many unrealized parental hopes. Needless to say, they became profoundly anxious because of the ideals of perfection given them by their parents, and uncertain if they achieve these ideals. What may have appeared as indulgence on the part of the parents was actually the exact opposite. Their parents used the child to meet their own needs. The imposition of these exaggerated parental expectations greatly confused the child about his or her actual abilities, which lead to the creation of their delusory beliefs about self.

Such unrealistic beliefs may provide the original impetus that differentiates the self-deceptive narcissist from others. In some instances, the child is unusually talented and motivated and is able to achieve the level of success consistent with the parent's exaggerated expectations. In other instances, the child has less talent or opportunities and utilizes the exaggerated parental expectations as the basis for excelling in some area of endeavor. In general, however, the self-delusory quality of the unrealistic beliefs created by parents leads to problems. An exalted self-image is usually difficult to sustain in the light of external circumstances such as disappointment and failure. The overvalued image of the self-internalized from an idealizing parent can become more realistic after interactions with more honest and critical peers, but the vestiges of the traumas of early disappointments tend to be indelibly etched on the fragile and distorted concept of self. Accordingly, self-deceiving narcissists are likely to suffer from interpersonal difficulties stemming from their desire to live up to the now-internalized parental illusions of self-worth. Thus, their emotions are superficial and their behavior has an ideal-hungry quality. In short, they find intimacy difficult and they look for others to provide structure to their lives.

Ministry provides a ready-made forum to reinforce and reconfirm their grandiose self. For the self-deceiving narcissist, the theological formulation of vocation as a "call" from God, a sign of "being set apart," serves as further reinforcement and confirmation of their belief in their inherent specialness and superiority over others. For self-deceiving narcissists with public ministries such as liturgical presiders, homilists, lectors, or choir directors religious services are viewed as a forum to exhibit that special call. Thus, the religious service is first and foremost a performance where the worshipping congregation "mirrors," i.e., admires and praises, the minister. Essentially, the narcissist believes that the real purpose of the religious service is "worship" of the minister!

Because of their self-absorption and self-deceiving tendency, narcissistic ministers must creatively distort the precept to love God and neighbor to fit their pathological perspective. For them, God, and everyone else, exists for one purpose: to love and take care of them. Their basic spiritual deficit is a lack of awareness of grace and an incapacity for gratitude. Not surprisingly, they imagine God as an all-giving father, and they perceive faith as magical entreaty. Consequently, they believe God will do exactly as they ask in their prayers, with no regard to the kind of claim God has on them. For them, there is only one kind of prayer: the prayer of petition or demand. Prayer as praise, self-examination, forgiveness, or thanksgiving has little meaning for them.

Some narcissistic ministers may have intense mystical leanings that pull them in the direction of mystical experience, including the occult. This is understandable in light of their sense of specialness and grandiosity. However, they are more likely to experience an exaggerated state of self-exaltation than a true mystical state. When prayers are not answered as they expect, they become narcissistically wounded and feel deeply rejected. As a result, they may reject God, becoming an atheist for an instant or forever, because God has let them down.

They are also likely to be insensitive to the suffering and needs of others. While they may help others in need and engage in acts of charity, they will do it only if their charitable deeds are noticed by others. If their efforts do not bring attention to them, they won't make a donation, extend a helping hand, lend a listening ear, or for that matter, continue it when the attention and praise of others stops.

According to J. Reid Meloy (1986), sexuality for this narcissistic minister, whether celibate or married, is basically autoerotic. This autoerotic preference is usually consciously denied but will be seen in a pattern of transient and multiple sex partners. Paradoxically, the narcissist's search for the perfect body to mirror the narcissist's sexual desire, as well as the desire to be young and attractive forever, may be accompanied by impotence. Without a physiological cause, the inability to achieve an erection may result from the narcissist's fear of dependency. Meloy points out that celibacy may support their autoerotic preference because they are allowed the freedom of sexual fantasy that has no limits or the imperfections, awkwardness, messiness, or inconvenience of actual contact with another person. Sexual images can be perfectly gratifying. Furthermore, Meloy contends that by requiring celibacy church authorities may be unwittingly sanctioning the narcissistic minister's preference for fantasy and masturbation.

To sum up this section, it is important to underscore that self-deceptive narcissistic ministers are much more approachable than their reactive counterparts. They are not nearly as exploitative and are more tolerant of dissenting opinions. They also appear more insecure. They are wary of threats in the environment and attempt to avoid making mistakes. They are not as quick to devalue others, are more eager to please, and are willing to engage in deals and exchanges with their followers. Their style of relating can have a more collegial quality as compared to reactive narcissists who are more concerned with how to transform those around them. The self-deceiving type stems from exaggerated parental expectations and demands, while the reactive type derives from harsh and brutal parenting. Although there are clear differences in the origins and relational behaviors of both types, both are preoccupied and dominated by their grandiosity.

In theory it is easy to distinguish between reactive and self-deceptive narcissism, while in practice the distinction is more difficult to make. This is mostly due to differences in parental response toward the developing child. One parent might have taken a cold, hostile, rejecting attitude, while the other might have been supportive, thus resulting in different gradations or mixtures of narcissistic styles. In addition, instead of being frustrated when ambitious parental expectations were incongruent with external reality, the child may have striven successfully to bring their abilities up to their perceived capacity. Furthermore, learning experiences later in life could have had buffering or mitigating effects.

### Constructive Narcissism

Constructive narcissists or narcissistic personalities do not behave in a reactive or self-deceptive manner, and because they meet less than five of the nine DSM-IV criteria, do not qualify for the diagnosis of narcissistic personality disorder. They seldom distort reality or use primitive defenses such as splitting, projection, or idealization, and are less anxious and estranged from thoughts and feelings. Instead, they are willing to express their needs and take responsibility for their actions. They tend to be confident and independent thinkers, largely because of parental encouragement. Furthermore, they were helped by their parents to see things in perspective and to avoid scapegoating and other destructive ploys. But most importantly, their parents' expectations of them were realistic and balanced which promoted accurate reality testing. When disappointed, these ministers seldom act spitefully, and are capable of encouraging others and engaging in reparative action.

Nevertheless, these ministers have learned the art of manipulation and occasionally act opportunistically. Still, they have the capacity to relate collegially with peers and those to whom they minister. They possess a high degree of confidence in their abilities and are highly goal-oriented. They will take ultimate responsibility for their decisions without blaming others when things go wrong. Still, they sometimes come across as lacking in warmth and consideration. Their sense of inner direction, however, gives them the ability to inspire others and create a common cause, transcending petty self-interests.

In summary, reactive narcissistic ministers tend to be ruthless, grandiose, and exhibitionistic. They seek to dominate and control and are extremely exploitative. Self-deceptive narcissistic ministers are less grandiose and exhibitionistic. They want to be liked and are much less tyrannical. Still, they lack empathy, are obsessed mainly with their own needs, and are given to being discreetly Machiavellian, that is, cunning and duplicitous. Finally, constructive narcissistic ministers are also ambitious, manipulative, and hypersensitive to criticism. Yet, they possess sufficient self-confidence, adaptability, and humor to be effective in a variety of ministerial situations and interpersonal challenges. Finally, because constructive narcissists are not personality-disordered ministers, they seldom create the havoc in their ministries that is the hallmark of the reactive and self-deceiving narcissists.

## Interventions with Narcissistic Ministers

For the most part, constructive narcissistic ministers engender little, if any, trouble in their ministries. But what can religious leaders and superiors do about the two more dysfunctional types of ministers?

### *Organizational*

The first step is to recognize the narcissistic pattern of exclusivity, empire building, and unrealistic expectations that inevitably leads to trouble and havoc. In situations where the religious organization or community is centralized and the reactive or self-deceptive narcissistic minister is dominant, poor performance and subsequent dismissal by a strong board (that is a parish council, provincial council, or diocesan executive committee) may be the only alternative. Even this option may be of limited utility when the narcissistic minister has significant influence over members of such boards.

It is very difficult to modify the narcissistically disordered personality, especially the reactive narcissist. When the trouble and havoc engendered by narcissistically disordered ministers becomes insurmountable there may be no alternative but to terminate or transfer them to reduce their influence, or stem a crisis situation. Certain strategies and tactics may be effective in this regard. For example with the troublesome reactive narcissistic minister, power and specific responsibilities can be distributed more broadly in the community or congregation insuring that more members can be involved in strategic decisions. Task forces, parallel structures, and executive committees can provide forums in which other ministers can express their viewpoints, while permitting narcissistic ministers to learn from and have their influence mitigated by others. Exclusivity, empire building, and unrealistic perspectives are thereby discouraged. It is my experience that establishing boundaries and limits with either reactive or self-deceiving narcissists is difficult, and the religious leader or board may have to raise the prospect of termination, transfer, or legal action if change doesn't occur, and be fully prepared to take that action.

Furthermore, preventive maintenance should be a top priority. A strategic plan should be developed by all religious communities and organizations to modify procedures for recruitment, selection, and discernment procedures to screen out excessive narcissism. In business organizations, psychological assessment and psychologically-focused interviewing is an essential part of the selection process for many employees, particularly middle- and upper-level managers. The typical manager may undergo a number of psychological assessments over the course of his or her career, usually when being considered for a promotion or job change. Management has found this data inestimable in increasing the "fit" between employee and job, as well as in reducing losses and risk. Presumably, religious leaders would be equally concerned about the "fit" between a particular minister and a particular ministry. And, since the Church has recently become quite sensitive to the matter of risk and financial losses, identifying excessive narcissism is not only prudent, but demonstrates care and concern for the community.

*Psychotherapeutic*

When all of these possible interventions fail and the narcissistic behavior of the minister becomes extreme, outside professional help is needed, if the individual is willing to consider that alternative. Referral for individual psychotherapy is one option, but so is group therapy. Nonetheless, individual psychotherapy with the narcissistic personality-disordered ministers is long-term, time-intensive, difficult, and costly. Interestingly, couples therapy with the narcissist has been shown to be the most efficient and cost-effective treatment, and may be the treatment of choice for married ministers.

# References

Manfred Kets de Vries, *Prisoners of Leadership.* New York: Wiley, 1989.

J. Reid Meloy, "Narcissistic Psychopathology and the Clergy," *Pastoral Psychology* 35, 1, 50–55, 1986.

Len Sperry, *Handbook of Diagnosis and Treatment of DSM-IV Personality Disorders.* New York: Brunner/Mazel, 1995.

Len Sperry, "Neurotic Personalities in Religious Settings," *Human Development* 12, 3, 11–17 (Fall) 1991.

# 3

## Sexually Abusing Behavior in Ministry

He had been ordained less than three years before the first complaint of sexual impropriety was received at the chancery office. The priest had been assigned to a suburban parish where he quickly befriended a number of single women in that congregation. One of these women had just experienced a broken engagement and was devastated. She was a lonely, clinging female with few female friends. Furthermore, her mother had passed away when she was seven, and her father had died nine months earlier. Not surprisingly, she was depressed and unusually vulnerable because of these losses.

Father began "counseling" her, first at the rectory and then at a local motel. Besides requesting she not discuss their "counseling relationship" with others, he asked her to start wearing her hair down and he bought her two stylish outfits to wear to their "sessions." Four months later, the woman disclosed to her female spiritual director that she was conflicted about her sexual liaison with the priest. The spiritual director advised her to end the relationship and report the matter to the chancery office. When she attempted to stop the sexual relationship, the priest threatened to "ruin her reputation," and when he learned that the woman and her spiritual director had an appointment with the chancellor, he threatened her life. Thereafter, two other letters of complaint were received by the chancery, but both were quickly withdrawn.

When the chancellor confronted the priest with these complaints and the legal liability, the priest adamantly denied the claims and indicated he would be applying for laicization since he was about to be married. He, in fact, did marry another of his counselees. The wedding was quickly arranged in another denomination, and the couple immediately moved out of the state. His wife, as well as the first complainant, met criteria for borderline personality disorder.

The new pastor of a middle class, urban parish was besieged with complaints of sexual impropriety involving the congregation's flamboyant music minister. The complaints were filed by the parents of young adolescent girls who alleged the minister had fondled and/or kissed them on more than one occasion. One of the parish trustees had observed the minister touching one of these girls in an inappropriate manner at a parish picnic. In checking the minister's personnel file, the pastor noted that his predecessor had overridden the recommendation of the parish's personnel committee. In its background check the committee had learned that the minister had been indicted for first-degree sexual assault of a minor, but was acquitted of the original charge on a technicality. Nevertheless, he was ordered to refrain from contact with minors and to receive ongoing psychiatric treatment for at least one year. Subsequently the state revoked his teaching credential. Within six months he left that state and applied for the music ministry position.

In reviewing the criminal records, the prior pastor had rationalized that he wasn't too concerned since the applicant hadn't served jail time, and "besides forgiveness is the Christian way, let's give this guy a chance." The applicant was hired. No problems were noted in the first year, but by the end of the second year, two complaints of molestation were received. However, since this marked the end of the pastor's term, he left the matter to his successor stating: "I'm not sure I would have renewed his (the music minister's) contract this year, but I didn't want to leave you high and dry without a liturgy and music minister."

## Dynamics of Sexually Abusing Ministers

Both of these ministers reflect the dynamics of the sexually abusing professional. Both ministers are the type of impaired professionals that damage lives and wreak havoc in the organizations and institutions in which they practice. The term "sexually abusing" can be distinguished from "sexually abusive" in that sexually abusive is the more generic term referring to any instance of sexual violation. In this article sexually abusing refers to a sexual violation that is perpetrated in the context of a professional relationship in which the violation of a sacred trust occurs. Thus, the term sexually abusive would apply to the priest pedophile who hides his identity and cruises adolescent hangouts looking for some action, while the term sexually abusing applies to the minister, who relying on the sacred trust attendant to his ministerial identity, befriends an adolescent parishioner and subsequently seduces him or her.

This chapter focuses exclusively on the sexually abusing minister. There are at least three types of sexually abusing ministers: those who engage in pedophilia, those who are sexually dominating, and those who lead double lives. Patrick Carnes, Ph.D. (1989), believes that "sexual addiction" is the core dynamic for understanding sexual abuse. My experience is that this dynamic is present in many, but not all, sexually abusing ministers. This chapter briefly describes the concept of sexual addiction along with some other personality dynamics that relate to pedophilia and domination. It also discusses psychiatric and organizational interventions that can prevent and reduce their incidence and prevalence in ministry. Since boundaries and power issues are central to these dynamics, these are discussed in some detail as background prior to a discussion of the two types of sexual abuse.

Parenthetically, the most common context lay people have for relating to authorized ministers, whether ordained or not, is in a parish setting. Obviously, there are other contexts as well, such as diocesan offices and programs, religious communities, or religious institutions such as hospitals. For convenience, I will use the designation "minister–parishioner" to refer to all ministerial relationships between ministers and those whom are ministered to irrespective of context.

## Boundaries, Power, and Intimacy in Ministry

### *Boundaries*

A boundary is a point of separation. For individuals, the basic separation or boundary is between self and others. A characteristic of early infancy is the infant's perception of no separation between self and mother. In the course of normal growth and development, it is expected that the self becomes better delineated and that a clear boundary between self and others develops and is maintained. This interpersonal boundary specifies the degree of intrusiveness which will be accepted in the relationship. For a married couple, commitment to their relationship is a basic boundary issue, as is the partner's relative commitments to his job, extended family, friends and the private space to be alone with one's thoughts and dreams without intrusion. For example, carrying on an extra-marital affair would be a violation of this basic relational boundary. Boundaries can be rigid, clear or diffuse. Clear boundaries are considered to be healthy and functional, while rigid and diffuse ones are considered pathological.

Conversely, individuals who have grown up in families with diffuse boundaries are very likely to exhibit a poorly delineated sense of self, and they are also very likely to experience problems establishing and maintaining healthy boundaries with other individuals and with institutions. Thus, individuals with personality structures that are characterized by self-deficits and identity problems, such as borderline personality disorder, are likely to be victims of various kinds of boundary violations.

Professional ethical code requires that clear boundaries be established and maintained in doctor-patient and counselor-client relationships. Boundary violations occur when the counselor fails to set or enforce limits on the appropriateness of his or her own behavior or on the client's behavior. For instance, a boundary violation would occur if a counselor asks a psychotherapy client, who is an investment broker, for advice on a particular stock, or accepts sexual advances from a client.

*Power*

Boundary issues can become intertwined with power issues. Power includes responsibility, control, discipline, decision-making, and role negotiation. Interpersonal relationships continually involve overt as well as covert attempts to influence decisions and the behavior of the other person. Control or power issues are usually tied to issues of money, reward, and privileges. They can manifest themselves in more subtle ways such as escalation of conflict or one-upmanship in efforts to regulate another person's behavior. The basic dynamic in interpersonal conflict involves who tells whom what to do under what circumstances. Power in interpersonal relations can range from positive to negative emotionally, and from laissez-faire, to democratic to autocratic politically. Essentially, power becomes a meta-rule for all decisions about boundaries as well as intimacy. Power can be shared equally or unequally.

In a professional relationship, such as minister–parishioner, the minister is accorded a power differential. Even if a counselor or minister espouses mutual collaboration and decision-making, the power differential still exists. In other words, the client or parishioner still has less power than the counselor or minister by virtue of role and status. When this power over the parishioner is misused, it can also confound boundary issues. For example, when a minister makes sexual advances toward a parishioner, this behavior would be considered both a boundary and a power violation.

*Intimacy*

Intimacy involves self-disclosure, friendship, caring, and appreciation of individual uniqueness. It entails negotiating emotional as well as physical distance between significant others. In either instance, the goal is to balance a sense of autonomy with feelings of belonging. When issues of affection in a relationship become a source of difficulty, they can be manifest in various ways ranging from complaints such as: "You don't understand my feelings," to "I'm being taken for granted." True intimacy, as compared to contrived intimacy, requires that clear boundaries and equally shared power characterize the relationship. For this reason, true intimacy is seldom, if ever, possible in a professional relationship, given that a power differential usually exists. Thus, ministers or counselors who believe they truly love their client or parishioner are deluding themselves and others who become convinced of it.

## The Dynamics of Sexual Addiction

Based on his clinical experience, Carnes has described sexual addiction as repetitive, uncontrollable sexual activity ranging from pedophilia to extramarital affairs to exhibitionism. Sexual addiction is viewed as a variant of other forms of addiction. According to Carnes (1989), the individual with sexual addiction believes his most important need is sexual activity and that sexual activity is the only way for his basic need for love and nurturing to be met. In his work with sexually addicted clergy, Mark Laaser, Ph.D. (1991), a colleague of Carnes, notes that these individuals usually come from extremely abusive, chaotic families who are incapable of healthy nurturing. They view themselves as shameful, bad, and unworthy individuals who must earn others' approval, since no one will love them as they are. Furthermore, although they may possess reasonably good social skills, they have significant deficits in relationship skills. Thus, they have considerable difficulty with intimacy and tend to confuse it with sexual performance.

Laaser believes sexually addicted ministers constantly search for ways of reducing shame and guilt. He notes that many had hoped their ordination would have controlled their sexual desires and that taking on the role of minister would somehow alleviate their sense of worthlessness. Laaser contends that sexual addiction becomes entwined with the role of minister to form the identity of the sexually addicted minister. He has observed that these individuals utilize their role as minister in an attempt to manage their addiction, deny its presence, and minimize its consequences both for themselves and their victims.

My experience is that many sexually abusing ministers meet this definition of sexual addiction. In fact, such individuals often have two or more other substance (i.e., alcohol, drug, or compulsive eating) or behavioral addictions (i.e., gambling, workaholism, etc.). However, there is also another group of sexually abusing ministers, particularly those who are severely personality-disordered but do not exhibit other addictive behaviors, who don't seem to fit Carnes' and Laaser's characterization.

## Sexually Dominating Ministers

Unlike pedophilia, sexual domination involves two adults, more often of different rather than of the same gender. Sexually dominating ministers exhibit a recurring pattern of exerting significant control, emotional and mental as well as sexual, over another person. By definition, this excludes ministers who, in a time of turmoil, engage in a single affair, or who establish and maintain a healthy relationship with another.

The first case example portrays a sexually dominating minister. The dynamics of mental, emotional, and physical domination are noteworthy in this case. These include the priest's efforts to change her hair style and clothing, to impose silence on their counseling relationship, to threaten her physically and emotionally if she met with the chancellor, to exploit her vulnerability regarding the losses of family members, and to violate boundaries in their so-called counseling relationship.

There are several reasons ministers give to rationalize their behavior. These range from loneliness to sexual frustration to "becoming more sexually experienced to better understand and counsel married people" to "showing her that someone still cares." Of course, these are simply rationalizations that beg the question of professional ethics and the "sacred trust" inherent in minister-parishioner relationships. Violations of sexual boundaries and preying on the emotional vulnerabilities of another are never justifiable.

In the past decade, most states and jurisdictions have enacted statutes prohibiting sexual relations, even consensual relations, between helping professionals, i.e., physicians, counselors, and clergy, and their patients or clients. Furthermore, related professional organizations have enacted ethical standards regarding intimacy and sexual impropriety in professional relationships.

Are all sexual relationships between ministers and parishioners inappropriate? The answer is yes. When an individual functions in the role of minister, he or she is usually perceived as "set apart," as representing God, and worthy of special consideration. As such, there is a power differential between minister and parishioner. This power differential can complicate boundary issues between minister and parishioner, especially if the parishioner has diffuse boundaries. Even highly functional parishioners who are under considerable stress can be vulnerable to boundary violations by a minister who "is manifesting the love of God" in a time of need.

Even when the minister does not function or represent himself or herself in the role of minister, such as when meeting someone on a vacation, relationship dynamics involving boundaries and power may still be complicated.

Is there a characteristic profile of the sexually-dominating minister? There is mounting evidence that ministers who engage in sexually dominating behavior have a predictable personality style and a predilection for preying on certain types of victims. Conrad Weiser, Ph.D. (1994), describes a profile of the sexually dominating minister. Based on his clinical data, Weiser concludes that ministerial sexual domination usually involves two individuals with severe personality disorders. The minister tends to exhibit either a borderline personality disorder or a low-functioning narcissistic personality disorder with borderline features. While these sexually-dominating, borderline ministers often report being sexually abused themselves, usually early in life by other ministers, they will "justify" their sexual acting-out on the grounds that they are "making amends" for the hurt they suffered. This "talionic" or "eye for an eye" mode of moral thinking is characteristic of the borderline personality. The talionic principle is a primitive way of thinking that is consistent with the primitive defense mechanisms of splitting and projective identification commonly utilized by borderline individuals. Not only is this principle incompatible with the Christian principle of forgiveness, but it complicates the rehabilitation process. The implications of this characteristic way of thinking and acting is described in more detail in chapter 5: "Borderline Behavior in Ministry."

Victims also tend to manifest a borderline personality disorder or a low-functioning dependent personality disorder with borderline features. Since boundary issues are commonplace in the borderline personality, and sexually dominating behavior typically involves boundary violations, Weiser's profile appears to have considerable face validity.

## Pedophilic Ministers

Pedophilia is categorized in DSM-IV as a paraphilia, or sexual deviation. Essentially, paraphilias involve recurrent, intense sexually arousing fantasies, sexual urges, or acting out sexual behaviors. Technically, pedophilia involves sexual activity between an adult and a child who is usually younger than thirteen, but sometimes is an adolescent. It appears to be primarily a disorder of men. Pedophilic activities can include undressing, masturbation or oral sex on the child, or penetration with mouth, vagina or anus with one's finger, penis or foreign object. The victim may be someone related to or known by the perpetrator, or could be a stranger.

Usually, the adult perpetrating the offense does not have a homosexual orientation. However, among priest pedophilics, it has been noted that the majority are homosexual or bisexual, with only about one-fourth being heterosexual. It is estimated that approximately 2 percent of priests meet criteria for pedophilia, which is about the same prevalence as in the general population. Psychiatric evaluation suggest that these individuals have significant developmental deficits, not only psychosexually, but in other areas as well. For example, they tend to have empathic deficits, meaning that they find it difficult to understand how others perceive and feel about a situation. While ministers are more intelligent and better educated than adolescents, they are also more likely to be psychosexually confused, be "defensive intellectualizers" and exhibit only a single paraphilia as compared to other pedophiles.

There is also a group of ministers who are sexually preoccupied with adolescent boys or girls, but only occasionally act out these impulses. In other words, while they can exert some control over their impulses to act out with adolescents, they tend to be obsessed with pornography and engage in compulsive masturbation. It is estimated that this group is twice as large as those meeting full criteria for the disorder. While these ministers do not pose the same type of threat or liability as the full-criteria pedophilics, they are nevertheless a source of major concern to diocese and religious congregations.

The impulse to act out sexually with minors can be described as either "fixated" or "regressed." Fixated types have been noted to experience no erotic attraction toward adults and are likely to have been psychosexually arrested as young children. They are most likely to victimize boys rather than girls. They typically begin acting out sexually when they are adolescents and they seldom marry. Regressed types, on the other hand, are men who find both adults and children sexually appealing and have a preference for female victims. They are most likely to begin acting out sexually as adults. The trigger for this is a sexually stressful situation with another adult. This type is sometimes married or otherwise has functioned heterosexually. Both types are likely to have been abused as children.

**Interventions: Psychiatric**

Individual psychotherapy is often the first option that religious leaders consider for both pedophilia and sexual domination. In some instances it is an appropriate intervention. In most instances it is not, unless it is a focused psychotherapy that is combined with medication, group therapy, or in-patient or residential treatment. Most often, a diagnosable personality disorder is present which complicates the treatment process, and frustrates the clinicians involved.

There are some different focused therapies that bear consideration. One is the kind of sexual addiction therapy developed by Carnes (1989) and his associates which focuses on the individual's sense of shame and worthlessness in the context of an addiction's milieu. Another is a focused behavioral approach wherein the individual's sexual desire and subsequent sexual acting out is counter-conditioned. For example, each time the individual experiences sexual desire a whiff of a noxious chemical, such as ammonia, is inhaled so that a pleasurable stimuli is paired with an unpleasureable and painful response. Both of these focused approaches show much promise, although research results are mixed.

There are a number of medications that have shown some promise, particularly with pedophilia. One class of drugs called antiandrogens have been shown to suppress sexual arousal, fantasy, and sexual behavior. The earliest of this group of medications, Depo-Provera, required injection on a weekly basis and had a number of side effects which can affect compliance. A much newer medication in this class, Androcur, reportedly has greater efficacy than Depo-Provera with fewer side effects. Another class of medication, the selective serotonin reuptake inhibitors, such as

Prozac and Paxil have also shown some promise in suppressing sexual arousal regarding unconventional or deviant sexual behavior while preserving normal arousal. The advantage to this class of medications is that they are available in pill form and can be taken orally. Nevertheless, with any of these medications, the minister must have sufficient motivation to change and agree to comply with the dosing regimen. The wish to return to highly gratifying sexual activity is a major reason for non-compliance. Thus, it is not surprising that many sexual offenders seldom make this commitment voluntarily, which may then be court ordered.

The issue with medications is not only one of compliance with the drug regimen, but also a moral and ethical issue. The issue is one of free will: can and should a religious leader order a minister to undergo weekly injections or take daily medication to control a natural, human process? Some bishops and provincials are very reluctant to give this order, hoping that some other form of therapy or spiritual discipline will accomplish the same goal and preserve the individual minister's freedom.

## Interventions: Organizational

### Screening

Formation personnel and administrators of dioceses and other religious organizations have several responsibilities with regarding ministerial sexual abuse. The first responsibility involves careful screening of candidates. Today, screening of potential ministers is becoming more sensitized to "risk management" issues such as concurrent psychiatric disorders, low impulse control, and medical and legal contraindications for public ministry. Traditionally, standardized psychological testing has been useful, but it cannot be the sole or main screening strategy. Clever individuals with severe personality disorders, particularly narcissistic and psychopathic personalities, can and have 'passed' the scrutiny of the Minnesota Multi-phasic Personality Inventory (MMPI), the Millon Clinical Multi-axial Inventory (MCMI), and other personality tests. It should be noted that most ministers who have been convicted of pedophilia were "tested" before entering the seminary or novitiate.

Effective screening requires careful, in-depth interviewing by seasoned individuals who follow an interview protocol. This protocol should include a structured interview of the candidate's personality structure, family and developmental history, as well as social history (school, work, and military experience). Since a personality disorder is a lifelong maladaptive pattern, clues of its presence will emerge upon careful investigation. Essential background information on the applicant includes a detailed formal application form that inquires about criminal charges and convictions, marital status, psychiatric history, and a year-by-year accounting of time since high school. This should be supplemented with specific queries about the applicant's theological views, spiritual practices, and sexual attitudes and behaviors.

A set of interviews with the applicant should expand and clarify the applicant's written responses to these and questions to ascertain the applicant's capacities and maturity to function as a minister. At least one of these interviews should seek to assess the applicant's level of emotional, spiritual, and sexual maturity. The interviewer will have to be sufficiently skilled to formulate a profile of the applicant's boundaries and boundary issues, power needs, and experience of and capacity for intimacy. When it comes to conducting such interviews, graduates of programs like the Christian Institute for the Study of Human Sexuality are a distinct asset to dioceses and religious congregations.

Routine background checking should be mandatory. This should include a checking for a criminal record, a query of the listed academic institutions, novitiates or seminaries attended, as well as jobs held to verify the accuracy of information on the application. At least five letters of recommendation should be required followed up by phone inquiries of at least three of the recommenders. Presumably, such a protocol will screen out actual and at-risk applicants.

### Reporting

The days of benignly looking beyond and ignoring a fellow minister's sexual abusing behavior are essentially over. It is unlikely that dioceses and religious congregations will ever again presumptively deny charges of sexual misconduct or stonewall investigations. Media coverage in the past few years has made it painfully clear that civil courts have and will continue to hold dioceses and religious congregations liable for the actions of their ministers.

A development that has had relatively little media coverage so far involves recently enacted "vicarious liability and negligence" laws. These laws are directed at liability against individuals rather than institutions or organizations. Essentially, under these laws a professional colleague can be held liable for the sexual misconduct of another colleague. If a professional colleague knew about or could have prevented the sexual misconduct, that colleague can also be held liable. While these laws have so far been directed at physicians' groups, it won't be long before they are directed at colleagues on parish teams and councils, provincial teams and diocesan staffs.

*Monitoring*

After it has been determined that a sexual boundary violation has occurred, and the minister is made to undergo a rehabilitation process, a formal monitoring mechanism is usually required to maintain the rehabilitation gains and prevent relapse. This might precede or follow a civil or criminal trial. Central to this monitoring is a written agreement of objectives for the rehabilitation process and restrictions on the minister's professional and personal activities, including limitations or prohibitions on contacts with certain individuals. Only those ministry colleagues and superiors who have a need to know are privy to the written agreement. A mature, trustworthy minister is assigned the role of monitor, and regularly meets with the minister in question, on a daily or weekly basis initially, and then biweekly or monthly later, to review the written agreement. The monitor also contacts designated ministry colleagues to ascertain the extent to which the provisions of the agreement are being kept.

*Policy Enactment*

Dioceses as well as religious congregations and institutions must develop realistic written policies about appropriate and inappropriate sexual behavior. The policy should include provisions about screening applicants for various ministries and specific policies and guidelines about a minister's involvement with parishioners, including informal and formal counseling. This policy statement must articulate the importance of clear boundaries and the consequences for boundary violations. It must specify the basis for reporting, internal investigation, due process, monitoring impaired ministers, cooperating with police investigations, treatment of complainants and victims, and consequences for violation of the policy, such as professional treatment, termination/removal from a ministry position, and so on. Needless to say, unless such policies are enacted and consistently upheld, ministry personnel will quickly realize that the policy has no teeth or that loopholes exist. Predictably, personality-disordered ministers will avail themselves of these shortcomings.

A number of dioceses and religious congregations have already established this type of policy statement hoping to delimit their legal and financial liabilities. This is an important first step. The next step is to articulate a policy about educating all ministry personnel about human sexuality in relationship to developmental psychology and religious and spiritual development. This type of policy is proactive and prevention-oriented. It should specify how formation personnel are trained, as well as how they will insure that all other ministry personnel are likewise trained. Some dioceses and congregations have begun this educational process by sending formation personnel to the Christian Institute for the Study of Human Sexuality.

## References

Patrick Carnes, *Contrary to Love: Counseling the Sexual Addict*. Minneapolis: CompCare Publishers, 1989.

Mark Laaser, "Sexual Addiction and Clergy," *Pastoral Psychology* 39, 4, 213–35, 1991.

Len Sperry, "Preventing Impairment in Ministers," *Human Development* 14, 24, 7–10, Summer, 1993.

Conrad Weiser, *Healers: Harmed and Harmful*. Minneapolis: Fortress Press, 1994.

# 4

## Psychopathic Behavior in Ministry

Recently, the *Wall Street Journal* reported that six major embezzlements have been discovered by the Catholic Church in the United States in the past three years. One involved a retired pastor being sued by his archdiocese to recover more than $200,000 allegedly misappropriated from his former parish for his personal use. Another involved the diocesan director of finance who embezzled over $1 million of diocesan funds, and then set the diocesan financial records and the chancery offices ablaze in an attempt to cover up the crime.

In another report, a priest being investigated for several sexual offenses involving young adolescents is found to have regularly engaged in sexual behaviors with persons of both sexes and of all ages. In addition, records showed he has several thousand dollars of gambling debts, over fifty unpaid tickets for parking violations, and four arrests for speeding in the past two years. Furthermore, when confronted by his bishop the priest admitted he had never told the bishop the truth in the seventeen years he had been in the diocese.

In another diocese, a choir director is reported to have conspired with a recently fired liturgist in forging letters of recommendation. It seems that a long overdue investigation of the liturgist turned up arrests for child molestation, the use of several aliases, allegations of other sex offenses as well as misappropriation of parish funds. The attorney for the diocese had told the liturgist that he was no longer welcomed in the diocese, that he should refrain from seeking any ministry position, and cautioned him that favorable job recommendations would not be forthcoming. However, this advice was not heeded, as the fired employee immediately sought similar ministry positions. In applying for these jobs outside that diocese, the liturgist falsified applications by indicating that letters of inquiry about his previous employment should be directed to the parish administrator, but the name and phone number provided was really that of the choir director. The fraud was soon detected. Because the job applications were returned by U.S. mail, both liturgist and choir director were indicted for mail fraud.

## The Psychopathic Personality

Many find it difficult to believe that ministry personnel could ever engage in criminal behavior like fraud, deceit, embezzlement or sexual offenses, but the fact is they do. Often these ministers are characterized as psychopathic personalities. This chapter describes the features of this personality type and how the Christian community is attractive to, and even protective of, such ministers who exhibit it. It also lists some corrective and preventive measures for dealing with these individuals.

The psychopathic personality is similar to the antisocial personality disorder described in the *Diagnostic and Statistical Manual, Fourth Edition* (DSM-IV). It is characterized by a persistent pattern of distorted ways of thinking, feeling and acting that can lead to disregard for and violations of the rights of others. The disorder is called antisocial because of the individual's proclivity to subtly or flagrantly attack social convention. There are basically three types of psychopaths: (1) the personable, superficially charming individual who cons others but usually avoids imprisonment; (2) the belligerent, antagonistic individual who openly flaunts social convention and the law and is likely to be imprisoned; and (3) the malignant narcissistic personality who was described in chapter 2. This chapter focuses only on the first type.

## A Profile of the Psychopathic Minister

Superficial charm, lack of empathy, and an inflated self-appraisal or self-centeredness characterize the psychopathic minister. These individuals view themselves as important persons and expect, and directly or indirectly demand, others to treat them as such. They need to be the center of attention, and when they cannot be they become jealous and despondent. While personable psychopaths spend much of their time trying to win the adulation and admiration of others by flattery and efforts to be pleasing, they are often oblivious to the feelings of others owing to their limited capacity for empathy (Sperry, 1995).

Furthermore, these individuals have little awareness of the distress they cause others by their deceptive and manipulative behavior. In addition, most are incapable of an intimate love relationship. For a psychopath an intimate relationship is merely a relationship based on satisfying material or sexual needs rather than one based on love and caring (Samenow, 1984).

Psychopathic ministers seldom allow themselves to experience hurt feelings since they believe that showing hurt and anger are signs of being weak and of being controlled by someone else. Thus, instead of getting angry, they focus on getting even—on retribution. Usually, they manifest their vindictiveness in a socially sophisticated manner. Because they don't experience guilt feelings, they can experience immense pleasure as they cleverly strategize a plan for "settling the score."

Failing to trust others is another core feature of the psychopathic personality. Since they have never learned how to trust their family, they cannot trust others. Many come from dysfunctional families in which one or both parents displayed psychopathic patterns or traits, were alcohol or drug addicted, or emotionally, physically or sexually abusive. As a result of being unable to trust his parents, the minister generalizes this distrustful attitude to all others.

Typically, psychopathic ministers are convinced that they must be on guard against others who will attempt to use and manipulate them. Irrespective of what others may do for them, the psychopath believes that personal gain is the only basis on which others act. Consequently, they have difficulty understanding the concepts of charity and self-sacrifice. For them, charity always begins at home.

Psychopathic ministers also have underdeveloped consciences. While they are aware of right and wrong and can discuss moral issues intelligently, they do not believe that any moral code is applicable in their lives. Consequently, they feel no guilt when violating such codes. The notion of sin is difficult for them to fathom since they believe that accomplishing their own purposes has more meaning than sinning. For instance, on his return from national conferences a liturgical minister brought back expensive souvenirs for selected female choir members. Concerned with the mounting "miscellaneous expenses" on his past two travel reimbursement vouchers, the parish administrator confronted the minister about these expenses only to discover that the parish had been billed for these expensive items. The minister angrily justified these gifts saying that since the parish was well-off financially it should be more than willing to subsidize his "generous spirit in upholding the morale of the choir." After all, he contended that because of his extraordinary artistic skills and an excellent reputation, the parish should be eager to reward him in many ways beyond his meager salary!

As already noted, these individuals are adept at manipulating and exploiting others. One way of controlling others is through deception and deceit. Personable psychopaths usually appear so poised and gracious that their honesty and sincerity is seldom questioned by others, at least initially. They can convincingly bend the truth and lie with consummate skill. They may use aliases or engage in malingering behavior. Lying and prevarication seem to be automatic responses that not only "solve" immediate problems for the psychopath, but provides them immense pleasure in conning unsuspecting and gullible religious persons (Peck, 1983).

These individuals are adept at recognizing and pursuing the trappings of power and prestige associated with high status and the upper-class lifestyle. They may be ingratiating, cooperative, and seemingly unselfish as they move up the ladder of the power structure. When they have achieved their position of privilege, they then focus their time, energy, and attention in accumulating the trappings of power dictated by this position. These can include discretionary funds, expensive cars, lavish living accommodations, and sexual favors.

In order to remain in these positions of power, they invariably surround themselves with sycophants who protect them from and inform them of threats and challenges to their power. Such servile individuals are easily entranced by the psychopathic minister's "holiness," apparent concern for them, and the sense of specialness they feel in being able to serve him or her. As such, they permit themselves to be easily controlled both mentally and emotionally such that the minister functions almost as a cult leader to them.

The essential spiritual issue with psychopathic ministers is their ingrained tendency to focus on the power, status, and control in their relationships. Their self-serving thinking goes something like this: because they must be in control of a given situation or relationship, God cannot really be in control. Therefore, they must be God! The psychopath utilizes several basic strategies for achieving this degree of personal control. Graciousness, cheerfulness, and charm typically usually provide them the measure of control and power they seek. When these strategies do not work, the psychopath can quickly and easily shift to coercion and mean-spirited behavior to achieve the necessary competitive edge or interpersonal leverage they believe is necessary. Not surprisingly, religion and spirituality become subordinated to their personal need to control.

Faith plays a rather limited role in the daily lives of psychopathic ministers. While some may extol their Christian identity and commitment, seldom do they practice what they believe. Other psychopathic ministers may experience times of enthusiasm and commitment, but seldom can they sustain this commitment. Subsequently, they shift from one spiritual group, movement, or congregation to another where perceived opportunities are greater.

Inevitably, these ministers exploit religion for their own purposes. For them, religion and spiritual pursuits provide a venue for acquiring power, money, or interpersonal advantage. Another motivation for "practicing" their religion or becoming involved in spiritual activities, is that others will view them as pious and upright individuals or as generous benefactors. Needless to say, acquiring such a reputation is immensely gratifying for psychopaths. When these seemingly pious and personable psychopathic ministers become involved in religious projects, they can manifest unfailing enthusiasm. Typically, this enthusiasm wanes as time passes and few persevere unless they continually receive adulation and praise for their involvement.

Not surprisingly, there is little depth to the spirituality of these individuals. They tend to relate to God in the same superficial and pragmatic way they relate to others. They are likely to image God similar to the way they experienced other father figures in their lives: as powerful, cunning, or ruthless. Often, fear of eternal damnation is their basic motivation for such religious observances as prayer or attending and officiating at services. While this fear may be sufficiently strong to deter them from committing violent acts against others, it does not preclude their use of manipulation and coercion. Prayer tends to be viewed as a means of informing God of their personal needs and wants. When their prayers are not answered to their satisfaction, they are likely to react with anger and resentment, and either stop praying or displace their anger on others.

## Clinical and Pastoral Implications

There are several actions that formation staff and administrators of religious organizations can take to correct and prevent the turmoil generated by psychopathic ministers. The first action is careful screening of candidates. It goes without saying that careful screening is mandatory for entry into ministry preparation programs, but careful screening is also essential in filling ministry positions. Although many religious Orders and dioceses acknowledge the value of psychological testing of applicants for the religious life, priesthood and permanent diaconate, relying on the results of a generic psychological battery is foolhardy. Clever individuals with severe personality disorders, particularly narcissistic and psychopathic personalities, can and have passed the scrutiny of the MMPI, for example. Witness the number of ministers who have been convicted of pedophilia and embezzlement who were "tested" before entering the seminary.

Effective screening requires careful, in-depth interviewing by seasoned individuals who follow an interview protocol. This protocol should include a structured interview of the candidate's personality structure, family and developmental history, as well as social history (school, work, and military experience). Since the psychopathic personality is a lifelong maladaptive pattern, clues of its presence will emerge upon careful investigation. At least five letters of recommendation should be required followed up by phone inquiries of at least two of the recommenders. Routine background checks of previous schools or seminaries attended or jobs held is prudent if any of the features of the personable form of psychopathy: charm, inflated self-appraisal, or empathic deficits are noted anywhere during the screening process. Presumably, such a protocol will screen out actual and at-risk individuals.

The second action involves regular reviews of the minister or minister-in-training's performance whether they are at-risk or not. Just as six-month performance appraisals are utilized in the business sector, these reviews are important to maintaining and increasing quality service in all areas of ministry. While it is commendable that some dioceses have adopted a variant of this appraisal system for recognized offenders, i.e., weekly or monthly monitoring of ministers who are indicted as sexual predators, some appraisal system or method needs to be implemented with any other at-risk individuals.

Third, psychopathic behavior needs to be addressed when it occurs for purposes of containing, correcting, and preventing it. The value of a diocesan-wide, semi-annual performance appraisal system is that individual ministers and their supervisors can more conscientiously focus on areas of improvement that become performance standard for that minister. The record of these performance standards should then be reviewed when annual ministry contracts are up for renewal, which again allows for any corrective actions.

Finally, the fact that psychotherapy and psychiatric treatment is mentioned last reflects the potential efficacy of the three previously mentioned actions or strategies. Psychiatric treatment and individual psychotherapy, in particular, have been shown to be minimally effective, at best, with psychopathic and antisocial personalities. Generally, residential treatment programs and homogeneous group therapy—a group consisting of ministers with severe narcissistic and/or psychopathic personalities—appear to be somewhat more effective than individual therapy. However, termination of ministry responsibilities is often the only realistic option in contending with psychopathic ministers.

## References

M. Scott Peck, *People of the Lie: The Hope for Healing Human Evil.* New York: Simon & Schuster, 1983.

Stanton Samenow, *Inside the Criminal Mind.* New York: Times Books, 1984.

Len Sperry, *Handbook of Diagnosis and Treatment of DSM-IV Personality Disorders.* New York: Brunner/Mazel, 1995.

# 5

## Borderline Behavior in Ministry

The pastor of a suburban parish was called to a meeting with the chancellor of the diocese to discuss a formal request for the diocese to sponsor a new Order of religious women. The written request noted that the pastor "has helped us discern the Lord's will for us to be formally recognized in this diocese and has offered to support us spiritually and financially." The chancellor wanted to know what the pastor's experience had been with Sister Joan, and he was most curious about the "offer" of financial support. He noted that over the past year two pastors had complained that a Sister Joan was actively seeking "benefactors" in their parishes.

The offer of financial support and complaints about the nun surprised the pastor. While it was true that she had mentioned her desire to establish a religious Order with a ministry directed to sexually abused women, the pastor had listened empathically and showed interest but made no commitment. He knew relatively little about her other than that she was on leave from her religious Order to "heal the wounds" of her sexual-abuse and gender-identity issues, and had met the other three women in a sexual-abuse support group. While he was somewhat taken back by her clinging and neediness, he was deeply moved by her story: she had left home to escape repeated sexual abuse, joined a religious Order at age eighteen, and suffered years of being victimized sexually by an older nun who had been her spiritual director. Some two weeks before he had reluctantly agreed he would consider her request to serve as their unofficial chaplain while they were in the process of discerning their future. But, he had denied her request to house her group in an unused section of the parish rectory. She was deeply disappointed and tearful by his decision. Her parting words were that she was on her way to a seven-day directed retreat.

The chancellor was also concerned about another matter, which involved the coordinator of Rite of Christian Initiation of Adults (RCIA) programs. Even though this divorced lay woman had excellent credentials and came highly recommended to this diocesan position, her performance over the past two years was lackluster, at best. She had the annoying habit of being either absent or late for diocesan meetings and appointments, even for a meeting with the bishop. Furthermore, she was inconsistent in meeting deadlines as well as in supervising her staff. Her first year's performance appraisal was below average, but her contract was renewed after she made an impassioned appeal to her boss, the diocesan administrator, citing the death of her grandmother as an extenuating circumstance. He agreed to renew her contract if she made a commitment to regular coaching with him. The coaching turned out to be an ordeal for him.

Recently, quite by coincidence, he had learned that the reason she had received positive references from her previous diocese was because "they wanted to get her out of that diocese before she caused anymore trouble." Apparently, she had been asked to resign after losing her temper at a budget meeting and screaming at the bishop that if he really cared about her and her program, he wouldn't cut her budget. Equally disturbing was that the director of family ministries of that diocese reported that he and his family were being "stalked" by her. Apparently, she had made late night crank calls to his home, had threatened to expose him, and spread rumors that he was having an affair with her. A shy and retiring but handsome man, he had been embarrassed by the attention she had lavished on him. After he rejected her offer to be his soul mate and divorce his wife and marry her, the harassment began.

## Borderline Personality Dynamics

In both instances, the diocese was contending with a phenomenon called borderline personality disorder. The borderline minister is easily recognized by a pattern of emotional instability and relational extremes. Unfortunately, this personality pattern is becoming increasingly present and troublesome in religious settings. Appearing emotionally stable at one moment, the borderline personality can suddenly become intensely angry, depressed, anxious, or questioning in regard to identity, goals, and values. Impulsive, unpredictable, and intense verbal outbursts and threats, as well as physical displays of temper or self-damaging acts, including suicide attempts and self-mutilation, are characteristic of this personality. Surprisingly, this emotional reactivity or liability tends to be short-lived. After that the person calms down, and tends to behave as if nothing unusual had happened. Characteristically unstable in relationships, the borderline individual sometimes over-idealizes another person, viewing that individual as incapable of any wrong— yet when frustrated with that person, he or she devalues that individual in the next instant (Sperry, 1995).

Borderline ministers have an intense fear of being alone, because when they are alone they feel incredibly empty and worthless. They can be clinging, dependent, and demanding that others should meet all their unmet needs. When others are unable or unwilling to meet these overly exaggerated expectations, the borderline personality may become enraged. Nevertheless, these individuals can be creative, intelligent, and emotionally perceptive and can function at high levels when expectations are clear and structured.

The borderline personality, more commonly observed among women, seems to be increasing as a diagnostic entity, probably due to increased family instability during the past three decades. This disorder tends to be exceedingly common in individuals with a history of severe physical, emotional and/or sexual abuse, or other severe childhood traumas. A number of co-morbid conditions such as an eating disorder, drug or alcohol abuse, depression, or chronic suicidal ideation and gestures are common with this personality disorder.

After hearing this description, religious leaders will immediately recognize and identify individuals on their ministry team or organization with borderline personality. A smaller religious organization may have one borderline minister, while larger ones are likely to have several. Even one person with this disorder can negatively impact the entire organization. Religious organizations with an emphasis on love and acceptance can expect to attract individuals who struggle with feelings of emptiness and isolation. Initially, the borderline personality may appear guarded in such a setting. As the organization persists in love and acceptance, however, the borderline minister will form intense attachments. This individual may give glowing testimony to the group's concern and hospitality, and they will predictably respond by giving even more of themselves.

As the demands of the borderline personality increase, the organization begins to feel controlled, manipulated, or trapped and predictably withdraws from these individuals. In response to what they perceive as a rejection and the possible loss of the relationship, they may offer to do anything, or accept nearly any humiliation or abuse to save the relationships and avoid the dread and pain of rejection. In anticipation of the threat of rejection, borderlines utilize a variety of psychological defensive maneuvers, particularly the primitive defense of "splitting." Since they have difficulty tolerating both negative and positive feelings simultaneously for the same person, they tend to view others as either all good or all bad. Not surprisingly, those deemed "bad" become targets for the borderline's emotional outbursts.

Overwhelming personal charm is another defense they utilize. To win and maintain the emotional support of others, they may lavish these individuals with gifts, time, or praise. Similarly, borderline females may use flattery or seductiveness to secure the attention of male leaders or those who are otherwise influential in the religious organization. When others do not respond as they expect, borderlines will experience feelings of abandonment and worthlessness.

How does this personality develop? The borderline minister often has a history of childhood abuse and trauma; the mother is often absent, neglectful, or in other ways emotionally unavailable or unpredictable. As a result, the child does not develop a secure sense of the mother as a good and caring figure. For the borderline, good and bad feelings have not been integrated. The normal process of development allows a child to experience both good and bad, black and white; the borderline personality has not had this integrative experience. Subsequently, rage remains unmitigated by love, and in the face of emotional turmoil other people are perceived as either all good or all bad.

The borderline minister tends to feel, "I don't know who I am or where I'm going," and so has identity problems involving self, gender, career, and basic values. This personality's view of the world is, "People are great; no, they are not. Having goals is good; no, it is not. If life doesn't go my way, I can't tolerate it." The basic life strategy becomes, "Keep all options open. Don't commit to anything. Reverse roles and vacillate in thought and feeling when under attack." The parental injunction internalized by the borderline personality in childhood was, "If you grow up and leave me, bad things will happen to me" (Sperry, 1995).

## Spiritual and Religious Dynamics

Predictably, borderline ministers tend to be as confused about the nature and presence of God as they are about their own identity and purpose in life. Not surprisingly, borderline personalities have difficulty maintaining constancy in their spiritual lives. As in other relationships, they are likely to view God as "all good" and themselves as "all bad." As such, they have difficulty dealing with their feelings toward God. Not surprisingly, their image of God can be as variable as their moods. When they are elated, God is imaged as kindly and beneficent, but when they are angry and depressed, God is imaged as a tyrant and source of all their problems. Because of their propensity to project blame outside themselves, they will harbor rageful thoughts and feelings against God and their religious organization even though they are extremely hesitant about admitting they harbor such thoughts and feelings.

Normally mild-mannered, higher functioning borderline ministers are occasionally observed to engage in vengeful behaviors, such as vitriolic character assassinations and summarily firing a parish council member over what others would consider a trivial matter. What accounts for such un-Christian-like actions? James Masterson, M.D. (1991), has studied the moral thinking process and behaviors of borderline individuals and indicates that they utilize the "talionic principle" in guiding their moral behavior.

This principle or *lex talionis* is the principle of retributive justice based on the Mosaic Law of "eye for an eye, tooth for a tooth." This revengeful, retribution-based moral code, which is more primitive than the Christian moral code of forgiveness, is consistent with the primitive splitting defense so characteristic of this personality disorder. In the movie *Fatal Attraction,* the borderline personality-disordered character played by Glenn Close "gets even" with the character played by Michael Douglas by pouring acid on his car, disclosing their affair to Douglas's wife, and then cooking his daughter's pet rabbit on the family's stove. These vengeful behaviors are in retribution for Douglas's rejecting her. Needless to say, borderline ministers have difficulty with the Christian concept of forgiveness. There are some profound implications of this avenging belief with regard to the borderline minister's participation in both psychotherapy and spiritual direction which are discussed in the treatment section.

Borderline ministers typically use spiritual discipline in a self-centered fashion. Prayer becomes a tool for getting God's attention. Their prayers tend to be exclusively prayers of petition: "Oh, God, get me that pastorate, so I can really love you," or "God, make the pastor care as much about me, as I do about him." In a childlike fashion, they may make all kinds of promises if their prayers are answered. When their prayers go unanswered, they are crushed and conclude that they will never be acceptable and lovable in God's eyes. God hates them they contend, because unanswered prayers means that God has rejected them.

Furthermore, their spiritual perception is greatly dependent on relational experiences with others. To the extent to which they regularly experience rejection, they find it difficult, if not impossible, to tolerate a relationship with God. Predictably, they will idealize a bishop, provincial, or district administrator as a kindly, loving substitute father figure. However, whenever this idealized individual fails to live up to their private expectations or because of some minor shortcoming, the idealized individual becomes the target of the borderline minister's rage and is immediately devalued. Since they have not learned to integrate opposite perceptions and feelings, such as love and hate, they are perpetually in turmoil, the kind of turmoil that affects most others around them.

Here is where relatively healthy religious groups and organizations have the potential for being the instrument of deep healing for the borderline minister. For it is only in such a context of a sustained and consistent atmosphere—a holding environment—of love and concern that borderline ministers can ever be able to experience God's love in a sustained way. The challenge, of course, is for such religious organizations to set realistic limits for such ministers and maintain these limits in the face of the borderline's instability. Unfortunately, there are relatively few seminaries, parishes, religious communities or diocesan offices that can consistently provide the kind of holding environment that borderline ministers need. Unless these ministers—or ministers in training—are fortunate enough to have this sustained experience, it is unlikely that they will be able to achieve a sufficient degree of healing and wholeness to function adequately in most ministries today.

It is for this reason that borderline individuals, even high-functioning ones, are such a poor risk for ministry positions. They are very likely to fail at all but the least stressful of ministries, which are those that have minimal work expectations and deadlines and even fewer interpersonal demands. Since the majority of ministry positions today are high stress, high-demand positions that require considerable interpersonal skills, borderline ministers are a poor fit for most religious organizations today. Nevertheless, borderline individuals are very attracted to ministry in hopes that religious life can make up for the early trauma and deprivations they experienced.

## Interventions with Borderline Ministers

### Screening and Selection

Three strategies are offered for dealing with borderline pathology in ministry personnel. The first strategy involves the screening and selection process. The basic question screening committees must answer is: Will we knowingly accept and encourage impaired individuals to enter professional ministries? The fact of the matter is that borderline personality-disordered individuals *are* impaired, even if they are high-functioning borderlines.

According to Conrad Weiser, Ph.D. (1994), a psychological consultant to ministry, increasing numbers of high-functioning borderline persons have joined religious organizations recently and many more can be expected. While screening committees occasionally fail to recognize borderlines, they oftentimes knowingly admit these individuals out of kindness, desperation, or with the hope they will somehow change. The financial and emotional cost for this decision is extremely high, and it is paid not only by the religious organization in legal fees and settlements, and treatment costs which are inevitable, but also by the emotional distress incurred by those who must live and work with these impaired ministers.

Weiser, among others, believes individuals with borderline pathology do not belong in a religious profession. Since there are few candidates for the priesthood, screening committees may gamble and accept higher-functioning borderline individuals for ordination. These committees fail to realize the degree of havoc ensured by introducing borderlines into the already-troubled system.

Another reason to exclude individuals with borderline pathology from the ministry involves a range of moral and financial issues involving sexual abuse. There is mounting evidence that ministers who engage in sexual abuse tend to choose victims with borderline personalities. According to Weiser's (1994) data, ministerial sexual abuse often involves two individuals with severe personality disorders. The abusing minister tends to exhibit a borderline personality disorder or a low-functioning narcissistic personality disorder with borderline features. Victims tend to manifest a borderline personality disorder or a low-functioning dependent personality disorder with borderline features. Needless to say, adequate and extensive assessment and the willingness to exclude these candidates should be a priority.

*Psychotherapy and Spiritual Direction*

The second strategy involves treatment interventions. There are a number of issues regarding psychiatric treatment of borderline ministers. Until a few years ago the prognosis for individuals with borderline pathology was considered guarded at best even with interminable treatment. Clinical lore suggested that basic treatment consisted of intensive psychotherapy—and perhaps medication, hospitalization, and sometimes residential care—for a period of seven to eleven years. Now, because of specialized treatment protocols and strategies, the prognosis for treating this disorder is considered fair to good, given intensive treatment over a period of two to three years. Michael Stone, M.D. (1993), indicates that borderline personality disorder has the same level treatability, i.e., intermediate treatability, as does the narcissistic and schizotypal personality disorders.

Stone's guarded optimism about the treatability of this disorder is premised on the treatment provider being a specialist in modifying borderline personality dynamics. It also assumes that the borderline patient is engaged in the treatment process. Many borderline patients have been 'in therapy' for years and continue to act out with suicidal gestures and other parasuicidal behaviors. Clearly, these patients have not yet been engaged in the treatment process. For it is only after the patient has sufficient motivation and commitment to change—and stop the acting out and other suicide gestures—that they can be said to be engaged in treatment.

It is, therefore, incumbent on those who have financial responsibility for the borderline minister's treatment to become informed consumers. This means recognizing that there are psychiatrists, psychotherapists and in-patient and residential treatment programs with specialized training and competence in treating individuals with severe personality disorders, and that most average therapists and treatment programs do not. It also means that since borderlines utilize splitting and other primitive defenses that competent treatment requires that there needs to be collaboration among those who live and work with the borderline minister and the treatment specialist to neutralize and redirect these devastating defenses. If the treatment provider does not mention or initiate the need for this collaboration, another provider should probably be sought.

Psychotherapy of the borderline minister can be either facilitated or hindered by concurrent spiritual direction. The extent to which these individuals can be assisted in establishing constancy in their image of God as well as in developing greater awareness of their talionic urges can greatly facilitate the treatment process. Because of their primitive moral perspective, their talionic urge to seek retribution for present and past rejections needs to be continually addressed both inside and outside psychotherapy. The basic choice that the borderline in treatment must face is "between getting better, and getting even." So many of the borderline minister's behaviors bespeak the message: "I won't budge for anybody," be it psychiatrist, spiritual director, or bishop, superior or provincial. The spiritual director who is aware of this phenomenon will recognize the various ways that talionic urges are manifest.

It was mentioned earlier that the borderline's primitive retribution-based moral code is consistent with their primitive splitting defense. It is also related to their propensity to engage in projective identification. In therapy or spiritual direction with a borderline patient, projective identification occurs when the patient projects some negative element of herself onto the naive therapist or director who unconsciously identifies with what is projected and begins to feel or behave like the projected element because of the interpersonal pressure of the patient. More experienced and self-aware therapists and directors deflect, confront or process these projected negative elements, thereby avoiding this seductive dance.

Unfortunately, most people are unaware of this projective process and too easily become hooked into this dance. As long as needy or angry borderline ministers continue to "demand" that everyone must "make up" for their abuse, lack of nurturing, and trauma in their early life, they will continually hook their ministry peers, superiors, and spiritual directors in this projective process. Not surprisingly, this demand is rooted in their talionic moral belief system: they are entitled to avenge others—get others to nurture them, to take care of them, to give them special dispensations—to make up for their perceived early losses.

They will want to discuss psychotherapeutic issues in their spiritual direction sessions, they will call unsuspecting colleagues in the middle of the night to talk about how bad they feel, they will "refuse" to take part in community reconciliation activities because they are "too fragile," etc. With borderline ministers, the basic task in psychotherapy and the basic task in spiritual direction is to confront their talionic code as inconsistent with Christian beliefs, and reframe their life's journey as getting on with their life—

meaning taking on the role of co-creator and forgiver—instead of getting even with life. Spiritual directors, religious administrators, and ministry colleagues who "put up with" the borderline's splitting, blaming, and projective identification, are not helping the borderline, but are reinforcing his/her pathology at great expense to all involved.

## Organizational Strategy

The third strategy involves organizational interventions. Setting limits and ministry team cohesiveness are two basic tactics that are quite effective in containing borderline pathology in religious organizations. Since borderlines have difficulty establishing boundaries and limits for themselves, others can and should help them in setting limits that are clear, realistic, consistent, enforceable, and then promptly enforced. Limit-setting usually involves three categories: persons, time, and things. For example, if the borderline minister has been known to verbally or physically assault parishioners or co-workers, a firm limit to reestablish basic respect is needed. There obviously was no effective limit setting—if any limits had been set—in the earlier mentioned case of the RCIA director who had stalked a co-worker. As far as setting limits on time, if the minister routinely is late or misses meetings, such a limit should be set. With regard to setting limits on objects or things, if the minister has a habit of failing to return, misplacing, or misusing others' personal or community property, limits must be set. Not to set limits, so as "not to upset Sister" is not only foolhardy, but robs that minister of the opportunity to learn responsibility, respect and consistency.

Since manipulation and splitting are characteristic defense maneuvers used by borderline individuals, these maneuvers need to be addressed systemically or organizationally. To the extent that a ministry team can function cohesively and communicate openly and effectively, the borderline minister's manipulations and splitting behaviors will have little negative effect on the team. Unfortunately, splitting has fragmented or even destroyed untold numbers of parish councils, pastoral ministry teams, and provincial and diocesan management teams. When an individual team member is told something in confidence or is asked to keep a communication privileged, team functioning may not be affected, but if it is a borderline minister who is doing the telling or making the request, it invariably will affect team functioning. Therefore, whenever a member of a ministry team exhibits borderline personality, the team must do everything in its power to avoid being manipulated or split as a team. When a ministry team adopts the policy that all information shared individually—by the borderline member—will be shared with the entire team, splitting can be averted. However, when the borderline minister has established a close relationship wherein another team member feels compelled to protect or rescue the borderline, the phenomenon of splitting may be impossible to neutralize without outside consultation.

**Concluding Note**

Borderline dynamics and pathology are increasingly common in ministry settings today. Whether this trend continues or not is largely in the hands of screening committees. Until it can be proved otherwise, a borderline minister should be considered an impaired minister. Depending on the degree of impairment, these individuals can be expected to have varying degrees of negative impact on the ministries in which they are involved. The prognosis for the psychiatric treatment of this severe personality disorder remains quite guarded unless the minister is therapeutically engaged in the treatment process and treatment is provided by a skilled and experienced specialist. Finally, ministry teams and religious organizations that have been unsuccessful in dealing with the borderline minister's splitting may need to seek organizational consultation help.

**References**

James Masterson, *The Narcissistic and Borderline Disorders*. New York: Brunner/Mazel, 1981.

Len Sperry, *Handbook of Diagnosis and Treatment of the DSM-IV Personality Disorders.* New York: Brunner/Mazel, 1995.

Conrad Weiser, *Healers: Harmed and Harmful.* Minneapolis: Fortress Press, 1994.

# 6

## Manic-Depressive Behavior in Ministry

Rev. James Allen, an associate pastor at a suburban parish, was well-regarded among his peers and superiors in his southwestern diocese. He had a reputation for being a hard-working and productive priest both in his parish which was his full-time assignment, and at the Newman Center of the local state university where he had a part-time assignment. Recently, he was observed to be even more active and productive. Within two weeks he initiated several ambitious projects, including program development and a capital fundraising campaign. These projects were not new to the pastoral team because he had thought about and talked about them for months. Then he seemed to shift into a decreased sleep mode and a stepped-up work schedule, and started operationalizing these very diverse projects all at once.

Since he was so resourceful and successful in his ministry few initially noticed that his expansiveness was getting out of control. But when he began to call some of his priest colleagues in the middle of the night, sometimes talking about the same ideas repeatedly, concern began to grow. It was during this frenzied period that he began binge drinking and became sexually involved with a former parishioner whom he had met at a bar. This last action sounded an alarm in the parish and the diocese, and the pastor and vicar for priests mobilized very quickly. Plans were quickly made to admit the priest in a private psychiatric hospital where he was first given lithium carbonate, which was soon changed to carbamazaepine. Within a week and a half he was discharged to outpatient treatment which included psychotherapy and medication management. He was able to return to a level of more realistic activity and responsibilities.

## Hypomania and Bipolar Disorder in Ministry

This case illustrates an ordained minister who for several years manifested a hypomanic personality that over a period of few weeks 'switched' into a Bipolar I Disorder, a type of manic-depression. While bipolar disorder is present in approximately 1 percent of the general population, it has a much higher incidence and prevalence among ministers, perhaps in the range of 5 to 10 percent. It appears that most individuals who experience bipolar disorder exhibit a characteristic biological predisposition or temperament as well as a characteristic personality structure or style. Hypomanic personality is the most common personality structure noted in individuals with a bipolar disorder. Whether an individual with this personality style will manifest the symptoms of a bipolar disorder depends on the presence or absence of various triggering stressors and factors.

Hypomanic personality and bipolar disorder, in its various manifestations, are commonplace in professional ministry today, just as they are in professions such as law and medicine, and careers which include sports figures, entertainers, politicians, and senior executives. This chapter briefly describes the dynamics of bipolar disorder and the hypomanic personality as it relates to ministry. It then offers various strategies for managing these conditions with regard to psychiatric treatment and organizational considerations within a religious context.

## Bipolar Disorder/ Manic-Depressive Illness

### Clinical Features

Until recently, bipolar disorder was referred to as manic-depressive illness. In the popular mind, manic-depression is understood as cycles of profound elation or mania followed by a period of deep depression. Actually, in psychiatric circles and diagnostic systems like DSM-IV, the presence of mania or hypomania is the defining feature of bipolar disorder. Mania refers to a predominant mood which is elevated, irritable, or expansive and which is of sufficient severity to cause marked impairment in social or work functioning. Several symptoms can be associated with this mood: hyperactivity, racing thoughts, distractibility, pressured speech, decreased need for sleep, inflated self-esteem, and over-involvement in potentially dangerous activities. Sometimes psychotic symptoms such as hallucinations or delusions may be seen in the acutely manic individual. Hypomania refers to an elevated, expansive or irritable mood that lasts at least four days and has many of the same symptoms of mania, but causes less impairment than mania (Goodwin and Jamison, 1990).

Bipolar disorder has a number of manifestations and three types will be briefly described in this chapter: Bipolar I Disorder, Bipolar II Disorder, and Bipolar Disorder Not Otherwise Specified (NOS). Bipolar I Disorder identifies an individual with one true manic episode. While there may be a history of depression or hypomania, such a history is not needed to make the DSM-IV diagnosis of Bipolar I Disorder. In Bipolar II Disorder there is a history of major depressive episodes and hypomania but no history of mania. Bipolar Disorder NOS is a category for an array of bipolar spectrum illnesses that do not meet criteria for such disorders as Bipolar I or Bipolar II. It would include the designation "hypomanic personality."

*Concomitant Substance Abuse*

When an individual is diagnosed with a bipolar disorder, it is very likely that a concomitant substance abuse or dependence disorder is present. However, it is not likely that this related disorder is formally diagnosed and treated. Research suggests that at least two-thirds of all individuals with a Bipolar I or II Disorder have a diagnosable alcohol abuse, alcohol dependence, or other substance abuse or dependence disorder. Many individuals with bipolar disorders have family histories of substance abuse or dependence. And, many bipolar individuals have a long history of self-medicating their highs and lows with "uppers" and "downers," irrespective of whether they have ever taken an anti-manic medication. The type of substance abuse or dependence is quite remarkable ranging from uppers such as cocaine, amphetamines, and prescription medication like Ritalin to downers such as opiates, barbiturates or prescription medications such as Valium, Tranxene, Librium, Ativan, Xanax, Percocet, Darvon, Oxycodone and other addictive medications.

Ministers are particularly prone to abuse such prescription medications. Ministers, particularly clergy, find it relatively easy to obtain prescriptions for these medications. Family physicians and even psychiatrists may be easily persuaded to write prescriptions that further complicate the minister's recovery. After all, "no one wants to see Father Smith in pain (or anxious)."

## *Psychodynamics of the Bipolar Disorders*

For Freud, as well as many contemporary psychoanalysts, mania is understood as an effort to stave off and deny depression, otherwise the superego would flood the ego and overwhelm it. Mania serves the purpose of reaffirming that the ego's injury has been repaired and the superego conquered. Since the ego has defeated the superego, impulse control is overridden and the manic or hypomanic individual experiences a tremendous and triumphant feeling of power and elation. Although there is something compelling about this formulation, there is no research evidence that supports it.

Research reported by Dorothy Peven (1996) suggests that mania and hypomania develops in predisposed individuals with a specific temperament and personality style. Individuals studied exhibited a biological predisposition or temperament that was characterized by high energy and a tendency to experience strong emotion, both positive and negative, including irritability. These individuals were rated as sensitizers rather than repressors and sensation-seekers rather than stimulus-avoiders. In other words, these were high energy, emotional individuals who tended to be risk-takers.

Their personality structures were characterized by a high need to please and impress others, as well as to set high expectations and standards for themselves. Because of a high need for achievement these individuals tended to push themselves to be successful so as to impress others and win their admiration. Nevertheless, they tended to harbor an inner, covert rebellion against this sense

of obligation to achieve. Yet, while they felt oppressed by this obligation, they did not feel confident to ignore it either. Therefore,
they lived with the feeling of not being good enough, and of not
having accomplished enough.

In other words, these individuals were ambitious people who
burdened themselves with inappropriate goals of achievement.
Their strategy was to impatiently lunge in the general direction of
their ambitious goal, despite a reasonably high probability that
their strategy would fail. Unfortunately, such failure did not end
their need to impress. Thus, while they are in a manic or hypomanic phase, they try to overwhelm others with their fantasies
and grandiose ideas and plans. Since this strategy does not allow
for gradual, straightforward movement, they invariably experience feelings of inferiority at their "failures" and withdraw in
"defeat." The reason for this is that they suffer from low self-
esteem and believe that they must be responsible at all costs. They
only allow themselves to see the world in concrete opposites. If
no grandiose success can be achieved, they conclude that only
dismal failure can occur. Instead of recognizing their goals and
strategies as inappropriate, they blame themselves for their failures. Therefore, while mania is their heightened attempt to achieve
impressive defeats, depression is their exhaustive refusal to participate in life when it denies them their achievement and leaves
them faced with the burden of achieving. In short, rather than see-
ing mania as a defense against depression, Peven speculates that
mania is an intensified protest against burdensome tasks in biologically predisposed individuals.

## The Hypomanic Personality

Several lines of research suggest that there are three personality styles that predispose individuals to Bipolar I or II Disorder:
narcissistic personality, cyclothymic personality, and most especially, the hypomanic personality. The hypomanic personality has
been a part of the psychiatric and psychoanalytic literature for
nearly a century. Recently, interest in this personality style has
been revived due to the clinical and research focus on both the
personality disorders and the so-called bipolar-spectrum disor-

ders. Unlike hypomania which is an episode of an elevated mood that must last at least four days, hypomanic personality refers to a style of personality—both character and temperament—that is stable, fixed and enduring rather than episodic. Currently, hypomanic personality disorder is not included as a distinct and separate diagnostic entity in DSM-IV, but it is included in the International Classification of Diseases (ICD-9).

## Clinical Features of the Hypomanic Personality

The hypomanic personality is consistently described in the literature as being characterized by: high energy, needing little sleep, success-oriented, work addiction, playfulness, and talkativeness, but also by defective empathy, impulsivity, disregard of limits, meddlesomeness, and a corruptible conscience. Salman Aktar, M.D. (1986), has succinctly described the clinical features of the hypomanic personality. He notes that their **self-concept** is grandiose and overconfident. There is a sense of specialness that they share with narcissistic personalities. Moreover, they tend to be cheerful and optimistic most of the time, and they have little doubt about their capacity to make things happen. Nevertheless, they are given to self-doubt and find being alone difficult. Their **cognitive style** is characterized as glib, articulate, and knowledgeable. They have a penchant for recalling trivia and enjoy punning and the playful use of language. Thus, although they may have a breadth of knowledge they may often lack depth in most areas. In terms of **interpersonal relationships,** they quickly and easily develop a broad network of friends and acquaintances, yet they exhibit empathic deficits. They also have a tendency to over-idealize others, which can easily switch to contempt. Typically, they foster one or two extremely dependent relationships with individuals who serve and care for them.

With regard to **love and sexuality** they tend to be seductive and flirtatious and are fond of gossip and sexual innuendo. Hypomanic personalities may be sexually precocious and promiscuous. Sustaining a commitment to an intimate partner may be difficult, and they find equality in such relationships disquieting preferring to be the dominant individual instead. In terms of **social adaptation,** they tend to be successful in their endeavors because of their energetic, workaholic style, and because of their capacity to be decisive and daring. In the process they may display questionable judgment in social and financial matters. Not surprisingly, they gravitate toward leadership positions. Unfortunately, they become inordinately dependent upon praise and acclaim.

With regard to **ethics and moral standards,** these individuals tend to be enthusiastic about ethical and moral matters, but can cut ethical corners and can be corrupted. In their enthusiasm, they tend to set high standards for themselves and others, though they may fall considerably short of them. Because of their fascination with all aspects of life, they can become particularly enamored of new trends in psychology, philosophy, and theology. Aktar notes that they may deliberately mock conventional authority.

## Comparison with the Narcissistic Personality

There is considerable overlap between the hypomanic and the narcissistic personalities (cf. Ch. 2, "Narcissistic Behavior in Ministry"). Aktar reports that both individuals display grandiosity, self-absorption, articulateness, seductiveness and social ease. Both utilize rather primitive defenses such as splitting and projective identification. However, they differ in important ways. The narcissist tends to devalue others openly while secretly envying them. On the other hand, the hypomanic will be openly friendly to all, but privately hold some in contempt. The narcissist tends to be less talkative and seldom utilizes compulsive humor as does the hypomanic. Furthermore, while both are ambitious and extremely active, the narcissist tends to present as steadfast, dedicated, and humorless in his pursuits, while the hypomanic will appear to be more playful, digressive, and suggestible. Finally, the hypomanic individual is unlikely to manifest the vengefulness, vindictiveness and "narcissistic rage" that is characteristic of the narcissist (Sperry, 1995).

## Religious and Spiritual Dynamics of the Hypomanic Personality

The religious belief and spiritual behaviors of the hypomanic personality are unique. These individuals embody a unique image of God, manifest a particular style of prayer, and manifest predictable religious behaviors. These religious and spiritual dynamics reflect their basic spiritual deficit which is a lack of awareness of grace and an incapacity for gratitude.

## Image of God

Hypomanic ministers tend to image God as an all-giving father whose only purpose is to love and care for them. As an all-giving father, God looks down on them with great favor. He will make all their grand plans materialize. And, He is there to admire their many accomplishments. Because God is all giving, they assume that God will answer all their prayers. In short, God's purpose is to serve them. They are on earth, not to serve God or others, but are instead privileged to be recipients of others' service. Not surprisingly, they understand faith as their response to an all-giving God, i.e., faith is the assurance that their needs and wants will be met, that their various projects will be blessed and flourish.

## Prayer Style

Like narcissists, hypomanics believe God will respond exactly as they request in their prayer, irrespective of the claim God has on them. For them, there is only one type of prayer: petitionary prayer. Prayer of praise and thanksgiving may be for other people, but not for them. In the prayers of hypomanic personalities, bad things may happen to good people, but certainly not to special people like them.

## Religious Behavior

Because of their self-preoccupation and the belief that God's purpose is to serve them, they are likely to be insensitive to the suffering and needs of others. While they can and do engage in acts of charity, it is for one of two reasons. First, the act is related to the accomplishment of one of their grand plans; that is what is important, not the disadvantaged little people that receive some benefit from it. Second, the charitable acts are performed because they will be noticed by others. However, if their charitable efforts fail to bring attention to themselves, they are less likely to make the donation, lend a listening ear or a helping hand. And, when the attention and praise of others stops, so will their charitable behavior (Sperry, 1995).

**Interventions with Manic-Depressive Ministers**

*Psychiatric Treatment Issues*

Basic to effective psychiatric treatment of ministers with Bipolar I and II Disorders is the three-fold therapeutic task: First, these individuals accept that they have a serious, chronic illness. Second, they accept the fact that they need treatment for this illness. And, third, they must make a commitment to actively participate in this treatment. This is called treatment compliance. The reality is that most bipolar individuals are not effectively treated, mostly because they are not actively participating in their treatment. Psychological factors account for this non-participation and these factors greatly influence their treatment non-compliance, particularly medication non-compliance.

While antimanic medications such as lithium carbonate, carbamezapine, and Depakote free most individuals from the severe disruptions of manic and depressive episodes, psychotherapy helps these individuals come to terms with the repercussions of past episodes and comprehend the practical and existential implications of having bipolar disorder. Although not all patients require psychotherapy, most can benefit from one of its modalities: individual, family, or group. The clinician can establish an emotionally supportive atmosphere, be cognizant of and focus on general issues related to bipolar illness—specifically dependency, loss and need for medication, and encourage the patient to express their concerns. Providing such a therapeutic relationship increases the likelihood of medication compliance, and sets the stage for formal psychotherapy should it be indicated.

Formal individual psychotherapy is indicated in the following situations: those unwilling to take medication in the prescribed manner, those who are suicidal, those in whom a personality disorder—such as narcissistic or hypomanic personality disorder—is prominent, and those for whom issues of dependency and symbolic loss are particularly problematic.

Frederick Goodwin, M.D., and Kay Jamison, Ph.D. (1991), indicate that issues of dependency and counter-dependency, poor self-esteem, problems of intimacy, medication noncompliance, and denial of their illness are major issues in psychotherapy of bipolar individuals. It seems that the traumatic experience of the disorder itself and the nature of treatment, result in the losses that dominate the individual's life. Accordingly, Goodwin and Jamison (1991) advocate focusing treatment on losses: realistic, symbolic, and unrealistic losses; fears of recurrence; and denial of illness. Realistic losses include decreased energy level, loss of euphoric states, increased need for sleep, decreased sexuality, and possibly decreases in productivity. Symbolic losses include loss of perceived omnipotence and independence. Unrealistic losses include circumstances where the antimanic medication and psychotherapy come to symbolize the patient's personal failure. That is, the antimanic becomes a psychological "whipping boy" representing other failures predating the onset of the bipolar illness. A major task of treatment is to help the individual understand and mourn these losses.

Noncompliance with antimanic medications is costly not only to individual ministers and their communities but to society as well. Individuals who fail to comply with medication have a rather predictable profile, and they tend to cite medication side effects, and numerous psychological factors as the reasons for their noncompliance. Individuals who are at high risk for medication noncompliance are likely to have some or many factors of this profile: They are likely to be in the first year of antimanic treatment; they tend to have a prior history of medication noncompliance; they tend to be younger; they are more likely to be male; they have a history of grandiose, euphoric manias rather than the Bipolar II presentation; they have elevated mood and fewer episodes; and they complain of "missing highs" when they are in remission of symptoms.

Clinical experience suggests that "missing highs" is the most ominous risk factor. Accordingly, the clinician would do well to elicit the individual's explanatory model, including what bipolar illness and its symptoms represent for them. Since mania or hypomania associated with bipolar is, for all practical purposes, an endogenous stimulant which can be quite addicting, the "high" is preferred to the "blahs" associated with medications. Noncompliance is the individual's strategy to induce mania not just when depressed but when faced with problematic decisions and life events. Since the negative consequences accrue only later, the individual may not easily comprehend how the costs of noncompliance outweigh the benefits. Similarly, for the individual who has already had a trial of an antimanic, the learned association between the use of the antimanic and the subsequent normal mood or dysphoric state, may come to symbolize a loss of innocence from prepsychotic to postpsychotic consciousness. Thus, medication noncompliance can represent an attempt to recapture an earlier prepsychotic existence, one not yet despoiled by mania or depression. Another important task of psychotherapy is to develop a relapse plan. This would include an assessment of external events and cognitions that are particularly prone to trigger dysphoria or hypomanic feeling, and a plan for reducing these factors.

## Organizational Issues with Manic-Depressive Ministers

The basic organizational issue regarding ministers with Bipolar I and II Disorders is the same as the basic three-fold therapeutic issue: acceptance of their diagnosis, acceptance of the need for treatment, and active compliance with treatment. Too few bipolar ministers have made a commitment to all three of these therapeutic tasks. While many appear to have accepted their diagnosis and the need for treatment, the third task is one that few are truly committed to. Keeping appointments with their prescribing psychiatrist and filling prescriptions may signal good intentions, but failure to take medications as specified, unwilling to begin or continue with ongoing psychotherapy, and the sporadic or continuous use of alcohol and various uppers and downers are harbingers of relapse and treatment failure.

It shouldn't be surprising that a 1991 study found that the noncompliance with bipolar treatment—or treatment failure rate—is 50 percent within the first six months of treatment and rises to 90 percent within five years (Schou, 1991). The direct and indirect costs of such treatment failure is astronomical. To the extent to which Bipolar I and II ministers have a concurrent hypomanic or narcissistic personality, the treatment failure rate reaches 90 percent or more. By virtue of their unredeemed grandiosity, denial and specialness which translates to: "Other people may not be able to do it, but I'm different. I can handle these symptoms, and no one will tell me otherwise."

This attitude toward their psychopathology is more than a psychiatric disorder. It is a spiritual disorder as well in that these ministers basically put themselves above God and their superiors and invariably jeopardize the safety and well-being of the Christian community by their defiance. It is for this reason that many psychiatric consultants to dioceses and religious orders endorse a stringent screening policy for ministry candidates. Such a policy would disqualify the majority of candidates with diagnosable Bipolar I and II Disorders and a hypomanic or narcissistic personality. Unfortunately, many screening committees do not heed such input.

With regard to ministers with Bipolar I and II Disorders, it is important for religious leaders to recognize that manic and hypomanic symptoms signal a minister's lack of internal control and the need for external limits. It is not uncommon for bipolar ministers who have stabilized to resent the lack of external controls placed upon them by their superiors during the active phase of their illness. External limit-setting is essential when it comes to the abuse of alcohol, recreational drugs, and addictive prescription medications, as well as spending money, late-night phone calls, hypersexual behavior and the like.

### References

Salman Aktar, "Hypomanic Personality Disorder," *Integrative Psychiatry* 6, 1, 37–52, 1986.

Frederick Goodwin and Kay Redfield Jamison, *Manic-Depressive Illness*. New York: Oxford University Press, 1990.

Dorothy Peven, "Individual Psychology and Bipolar Mood Disorder." In Len Sperry and John Carlson (eds.), *Psychopathology and Psychotherapy: From DSM-IV Diagnosis to Treatment*. Washington, D.C.: Accelerated Development/Taylor & Francis, 1996, 77–114.

M. Schou, "Relapse prevention in manic-depressive illness: Important and unimportant factors," *Canadian Journal of Psychiatry* (1991) 36, 502–506.

Len Sperry, "The Narcissistic Minister," *Human Development* 16, 3, 36–41, Fall, 1995.

# 7

## Obsessive-Compulsive Behavior in Ministry

Fr. Martin Briggs is the recently appointed co-pastor of St. Thomas Parish, the fictionalized central city church setting for the *Nothing Sacred* television series. Father Martin is a grim, no-nonsense cleric assigned by the diocese to "shake up the parish team" and to insure that doctrine is not compromised in the parish. It is quite evident that he has ambitions for career advancement in the diocese and views St. Thomas as a place where he can prove to the vicar and bishop that he has the ability to control and redeem what the diocese considers an "out of control" parish.

His first order of business is to restrict nuns and lay people from preaching at liturgies. His next effort was to refocus the pastoral team's energy away from social action concerns, like their soup kitchen program, and toward more traditional concerns such as religious education programming and a choir. He quickly makes it known that he is a stickler for clerical protocol and liturgical rubric. While he is very concerned with pleasing the bishop and vicar, he appears to have little regard for the feedback of his peers and subordinates. Not surprisingly, his leadership style is autocratic and he resists efforts at team collaboration.

Needless to say, Father Martin encounters strong resistance from the rest of the pastoral team. He emphasizes self-improvement to the team, and takes to videotaping and reviewing his homilies to improve his technique. His plan for shaking up the staff is to revise job descriptions so that those currently in some jobs won't easily qualify for reappointment. More specifically, he appears to be threatened by strong women like Sister Maureen, a vocal member of the pastoral staff, particularly because of her views on women's ordination, and he seems convinced that she must be replaced.

Sally Wingert is a forty-two-year-old director of religious education for a midwestern suburban parish of moderate size. She is single and a former nun with very definite ideas about what children and adults need to know about their faith. In the two years she has held the position, she has gained the respect of most parishioners and other members of the parish team. While she manifests respect and deference toward the pastor, she evinces an aura of superiority over the rest of the pastoral team. She openly voices her opinions about the merit of the ideas and initiates of other staff members. As the associate pastor once remarked: "Sally takes no hostages." The permanent deacons and the school principal who have endured her critical appraisals would not disagree. In short, she has cultivated a reputation for being a no-nonsense administrator who runs a tight ship.

She is a tireless worker who puts in long hours and expects the same commitment from both paid and volunteer teachers and aides in her program. The only substantive complaint about her has come from some parents of adolescent girls in the high school CCD program, who think the dress code she established for the program is too strict. While parish staff and parishioners admire their DRE, no one feels particularly close to her, and she does not appear to have a social life that involves the parish. Nevertheless, it was totally unexpected when she submitted her letter of resignation in May stating she would pursue M.Div. training "to prepare for the time when women would take their rightful place in ordained ministry."

### Psychodynamics of the Obsessive-Compulsive Personality

Both of these ministers exhibit obsessive-compulsive personality dynamics. Conrad Weiser, Ph.D. (1994), a psychological consultant to ministry, has observed that the ministry has traditionally attracted obsessive-compulsive individuals. However, he notes this changed in the 60s through the 80s when civil rights, antiwar, feminism, and ecological concerns provided a ministry platform to narcissistic personalities, who in former days would not have considered a ministerial career. Today, however, there seems to be a shift toward more obsessive-compulsivity and less narcissism in ministry.

So what are the psychodynamics of obsessive-compulsivity? Individuals with obsessive-compulsive personality are habitually preoccupied with rules and duties. Rules provide a sense of orderliness in their lives as well as a measure of control. While obsessive-compulsivity is not necessarily synonymous with a conservative ideology, it certainly is not inconsistent with it. Following rules and the established order is comforting to this personality, as it confirms their view that the world functions best when there is order rather than chaos, and life is gentle and predictable rather than harsh and unpredictable.

Individuals with obsessive-compulsive personality are also unable to express warmth and caring except in limited situations. They tend to believe that any spontaneous expression of emotion could be dangerous, and that the extreme expressive of emotion represents "craziness." Therefore, they keep their feelings under control. Even their cognitive processes are attenuated and rigid, lacking a sense of playfulness and flexibility.

They are highly oriented toward a life-style characterized by productivity and efficiency and are temperamentally and emotionally insensitive to others. Competitiveness is not uncommon in individuals with this personality structure. They can be rather single-minded in their strivings and when this combines with their righteousness, they can compete with a level of fury that is formidable. Obsessive individuals have a tendency to be perfectionists, which shows in their over-attention to details, rules, and schedules. Not surprisingly, they are often workaholics.

Interpersonally, they are often polite and loyal, although somewhat rigid and stuffy in their dealings with others. While they are likely to show respect and deference—even to the point of obsequiousness—to superiors, they tend to show relatively little interest in collegiality with peers and those who report to them. They seldom delegate responsibilities for fear that the task will not be done properly. Accordingly, they are firm believers in the dictum: "If you want it done right, do it yourself."

In western culture, a certain degree of compulsivity in one's work is highly esteemed and rewarded by others. But for individuals with obsessive-compulsive personality such cultural reinforcement becomes a burden and an invitation to workaholism. When these individuals are not working, they believe they are not being responsible and thus have no self-worth. Therefore, they must always be doing something. They must take work home with them, and even when they are on vacation, at the very least, they must stay in touch with their office by phone, fax, or e-mail. Since many obsessive-compulsives have also internalized the theologically-ridiculous dictum: "idleness is the devil's workshop," they also feel morally obliged to work compulsively.

Individuals with this personality disorder can be indecisive and poor planners of their time as a result of their narrow focus and concern with precision even when precision may be irrelevant. Indecisiveness can take several forms. Decision-making may be postponed, avoided, or protracted. For example, the individual may not finish an assignment because she has spent so much time ruminating about priorities.

Furthermore, they are inclined to be over-conscientious and excessively moralistic and inflexible about matters of ethics, law, or values. Although they may generally seem to be mild-mannered individuals they can become quite self-righteous and unpleasant when a pet idea or ideology of theirs is attached.

They may find it difficult to be generous in donating money, time, or gifts to others when little or no personal gain will result. And, they find it difficult to relinquish worn-out and worthless objects even when these objects have no actual or sentimental value to them. Generosity is not a high priority for them: they believe in conserving everything they can. They may have large collections of books or records or whatever. They seem to have literally internalized the belief that it's better to save things for a rainy day than to be unprepared and unprotected.

As children, obsessive-compulsive individuals tended to have parental training that taught them to be good and overly responsible in all areas of their life. The spoken and unspoken message they would have consistently received from their parents and care-takers—called the parental injunction—would have been: "To be a worthwhile person, you must do and be better."

Psychologically, they tend to believe: "I am always responsible if something goes wrong, so I must always be reliable, competent, and righteous." Typically, their world view is: "Life is always unpredictable and expects too much of me." Their basic strategy in life then becomes: "Always be in control, always be right, and always be proper." Unfortunately, such a life script is usually experienced as a mild to moderate challenge even when things are going reasonably well, but always as a severely distressing and overwhelming burden when life is not going well. Finally, they tend to be hyper-alert to criticism from others, and so can easily rationalize keeping an emotional distance from others (Sperry, 1995).

Not surprisingly, these individuals experience excessive guilt feelings because of their internalized sense that they must assume tremendous amounts of responsibility for life. As a result, they are chronically anxious and tense, and seldom are able to look and feel relaxed. They are seldom spontaneous and almost never euphoric, and they cannot live in the present because of their fear of what the future may hold for them. So, they are always prepared—like good Boy Scouts and Girl Scouts—for the expected and unexpected. Since they secretly doubt their ability to deal with enormity of life, they reduce life to its smallest pieces. They believe that by managing these small pieces, they will eventually control the whole. Of course, it won't happen this way, because life cannot be controlled. But, they religiously cling to this fiction. Thus, their lives tend to be characterized by a quiet sort of desperation, drabness, and worry.

## Religious and Spiritual Dynamics of the Obsessive-Compulsive Personality

The religious and spiritual dynamics of obsessive-compulsive persons, particularly ministers, is rather predictable and unique. These dynamics will be described in terms of the obsessive-compulsive's image of God, their prayer style, their experience of conversion and vocation, and their religious behavior patterns and ministry style.

These individuals typically image God as a taskmaster, judge, or police officer. Because of their early life expectation or demand—from parents or caretakers—to be responsible and perfect, these individuals come to believe that God holds these same expectations of them. The belief is that God expects great things of them and will judge them accordingly. Certain scriptures further reinforce this expectation. For instance, "Be perfect, as your heavenly Father is perfect," and the parable of the talents tend to be interpreted literally by these individuals.

It should not be surprising that the prayer style of obsessive-compulsive individuals tends to focus on their own faults, failings, and need for forgiveness. They will hear and say the words: "Lord, I am not worthy that you should come under my roof, but speak the words and I shall be healed," but they can only allow themselves to believe the first part: "Lord, I am not worthy," but find it almost impossible to believe that they can be healed and be worthy. Rather, they easily believe and feel that they are sinful and are not, and cannot become, lovable. The words: "You are my beloved in whom I am well pleased" seem directed at others, but could never refer to them. Parenthetically, one of the markers that pastoral psychotherapists look for as the obsessive-compulsive personality grows and matures, is their increasing acceptance of their status as God's "beloved."

As to the matter of vocation and conversion: In his clinical research, Weiser (1994) has found that obsessive-compulsive ministers believe they were meant to do something important with their lives. They often report that when they were in their late teens or in their twenties, they recall being on a retreat or at church that it suddenly occurred to them that the Holy Spirit had called them to the ministry. Such a divine calling is important for these individuals, since they believe that their work can be nearly anything but it must be supremely important. They look outside themselves for a sense of direction or confirmation. Weiser notes: "Then God, or a cross, or a revered religious professional appears and they conclude that God has somehow clarified the direction."

In their ministry, there are various ways in which obsessive-compulsive ministers function and behave. We will describe two levels of functioning: high and low.

## High-Functioning Compulsive Ministers

These individuals tend to be regarded as highly effective in their ministries, and may even be considered leaders in their field. They may win awards, get appointed to important committees and task forces, but for all their success, their lives are decidedly one-sided. In ministry circles, they are almost always viewed as over-achievers and maybe even as leaders, but they are seldom viewed as friendly and caring persons. They tend to be somewhat emotionally immature and are seldom satisfied with their lives. Although they may extol the virtue of living in the moment, they seldom, if ever, take the time to smell the roses. Their interpersonal relationships tend to be predictably remote and lacking in all but superficial intimacy. Yet, they have some capacity for deeper intimate sharing and risk-taking if they can let down their intellectual defenses.

## Low-Functioning Compulsive Ministers

Because of the extent of their inflexibility, perfectionism and indecisiveness, they are rarely—if ever—able to keep deadlines, or be on time for appointments and meetings. Overwhelming guilt feelings can further complicate their ineffectiveness. Because they feel bad they let someone else down, they may be too embarrassed to return phone calls, answer letters, or e-mail messages. Not surprisingly, this lack of responsiveness compounds their original irresponsibility, resulting in them being even more ineffective and more guilty. Needless to say, these ministers are exceedingly frustrating to work with. Paranoid features can also be present in lower functioning obsessive-compulsive ministers. Usually, this manifests as suspicious of other's intentions or projected blame. The minister can become quite convinced that others are watching or checking for him to make a mistake, or judging his personal behavior or ministerial performance. Needless to say, these individuals are not reliable and cannot be counted upon. Thus, superiors and co-workers tend to label them as "difficult" people because of their perceived irresponsibility and lack of cooperativeness.

Under severe levels of stress, these lower-functioning ministers can become obsessive about their specific ministry or religious matters in general. Initially, they can be filled with generalized anxiety. Then a recurrent thought or scriptural passage "convinces" them that they are spiritually lost because they have themselves crucified Christ. Or, they feel they have sinned against the Holy Spirit and thus cannot be forgiven. As a result they become agitated and depressed and refuse all measure of reassurance and comfort. They are usually beyond rational persuasion, and may be clinically depressed and entertain suicidal thoughts. Competent and compassionate pastoral care typically includes psychiatric referral, but it may also require changes in the policies and structure of the religious organizations to which these individuals belong.

## Scrupulosity: A Special Consideration

While scrupulosity is commonly associated with the obsessive-compulsive personality disorder, it is actually a variant of the obsessive-compulsive disorder (OCD), which is a DSM-IV, Axis I or symptom disorder, rather than an Axis II or personality disorder. Just like compulsive hand washing or repeated checking of a door lock are examples of OCD, repeated confession of the same sin—sometimes to several different confessors—would be an example of scrupulosity.

### Characteristics of Scrupulosity

Richard Vaughan, S.J. (1994), describes four basic characteristics of scrupulosity: (1) an attempt to perfectly follow specific moral prescriptions; (2) the fear of eternal damnation based on the belief of having committed serious sin; (3) little or no concern for failures of human weakness or venial sin; and (4) sometimes, overwhelming anxiety reducing the capacity for making a moral judgment as to sinfulness of a given behavior. I would add a fifth: that the scrupulosity causes marked distress, is time consuming—takes more than one hour a day—or significantly interferes with the individual's daily routine and ministry or social functioning. In other words, there is a marked difference between someone who is concerned about sinfulness and confesses once, and someone who confesses it twenty times over three consecutive days! Only the second instance reflects scrupulosity.

Scrupulosity can be manifested in the reporting of tiny infractions of rules and inappropriate behaviors to a confessor, pastor, or religious superior. But, probably the most trying expression of an overscrupulous religiosity is seen in such individuals' interpretations of certain passages of Scripture. The scrupulous individuals may focus on passages that are tailor-made to their private biases, yet these passages are test cases for the acceptability of their worth as Christians. To them, any contradictory testimony in Scripture, church tradition, or the promptings of their spiritual directors is irrelevant. In years past, when weekly confession was a common tradition among Catholics, over scrupulosity among them was unwittingly reinforced.

### OCD vs. Obsessive-Compulsive Personality

While it is possible for a minister with an obsessive-compulsive personality to also manifest OCD—scrupulosity variant, it is rather uncommon. Actually, scrupulosity is a rather rare form of OCD. Research studies suggest that less than 19 percent of all patients with OCD meet criteria for the obsessive-compulsive personality disorder. Unfortunately, writers such as Leon Salzman (1980) and Richard Vaughan (1994) suggest that scrupulosity is one of the many manifestations of the obsessive-compulsive personality disorder and imply that somehow these two separate disorders are actually one disorder. Probably, the basis of this confusion is rooted in Freud's famous case of the Rat Man. Remarkably, the Rat Man did manifest both OCD and obsessive-compulsive personality. Freud, as well as many of his disciples, prematurely concluded that there were two manifestations of one disorder. Today, we know that effective treatment of OCD—and scrupulosity—usually requires medication *and* behavior therapy. As is noted below, neither of these treatments is necessary for the obsessive-compulsive personality disorder.

## Psychotherapeutic Interventions

When it is adjudged that a minister's functioning is sufficiently hampered because of his/her obsessive-compulsive personality, psychotherapy is probably the first and only intervention strategy that comes to mind. The basic goal of psychotherapy with this personality type is quite simple: the individual becomes able to balance his/her capacity to feel with his/her capacity to think, to live in the present at least as much in the future or the past, and to develop the courage to be imperfect to balance his/her perfectionistic strivings. Clinical lore suggests that long-term psychotherapy—lasting two to four years or more—is needed to modify this disorder. However, focused, briefer psychotherapy approaches are offering a promising alternative to this style. Since psychotherapy is never context-less, and because the obsessive-compulsive personality style is highly prized in certain religious organizations, psychotherapy may not, in and of itself, be the necessary and sufficient modality of change.

## Organizational Interventions

A few organizational interventions will be very briefly described here. Perhaps the most important of these involves the screening of candidates.

### Screening

Screening committees would do well to recognize the inherent bias religious organizations have for the obsessive-compulsive personality. Weiser estimates that the majority of ministry personnel are a combination of obsessive-compulsive and narcissistic personality features. This combination is quite interesting in that seemingly opposite traits are balanced: while the narcissistic style is characterized by entitlement, grandiosity, and poor impulse control, the obsessive-compulsive style is characterized by perfectionism, fearfulness, and the inability to act spontaneously. Generally speaking, high-functioning candidates for the ministry who combine both obsessive-compulsive and narcissistic features have considerable potential for a variety of ministries. Certainly, they are preferable to low-functioning candidates, and probably to higher functioning candidates that are primarily obsessive-compulsive.

### Mentoring and Spiritual Direction

Professional ministers—in practice or in training—who exhibit strong obsessive-compulsive features should be urged to work with mentors or spiritual directors who have balanced or mature personality styles. Just as psychotherapists with obsessive-compulsive personalities are not good matches for clients with obsessive-compulsivity, much can be gained by the minister who has his or her obsessive-compulsive style appreciated yet challenged by someone with another view of self-hood and life.

*Organizational Policies*

Since a given religious organization may be largely populated with ministry personnel with obsessive-compulsive styles, it is essential that diocesan and provincial councils consider how current policies, structures and culture may unwittingly reinforce obsessive-compulsive pathology. For instance, when a congregation's culture is characterized by workaholism, competitiveness, and premature deaths of its members due to heart failure and strokes, there may be considerable value in revising policies and procedures regarding such considerations as criteria for advanced study and career advancement, as well as the manner in which the group's charism is operationalized.

## Concluding Note

It has been suggested that the obsessive-compulsive personality dynamic is common among ministry personnel and religious organizations. Many dioceses and congregations have been well served by high-functioning obsessive-compulsive ministers and retarded by those who are much lower functioning. The challenge for screening committees and leadership councils is to review their personnel policies and their organizational culture in light of their mission as the basis for personnel decisions about screening, treatment and possible change of organizational structure and policies.

## References

Leon Salzman, *Treatment of the Obsessive Personality*. New York: Jason Aronson, 1980.

Len Sperry, *Handbook of Diagnosis and Treatment of the DSM-IV Personality Disorders.* New York: Brunner/Mazel, 1995.

Richard Vaughan, *Pastoral Counseling and Personality Disorders.* Kansas City, Mo.: Sheed & Ward, 1994.

Conrad Weiser, *Healers: Harmed and Harmful.* Minneapolis: Fortress Press, 1994.

# 8

## Depressive Behavior in Ministry

An energetic, middle-aged pastor who had recently been discharged from the hospital for treatment of a mild heart attack was finding readjustment to parish life difficult. Two weeks before his heart attack, he had presided at the funeral of his younger brother. The two had been quite close, and the pastor chided himself for failing to recognize the signs of suicide in his brother. Following the hospitalization, the pastor began having difficulty falling and staying asleep. His appetite, energy level, and ability to concentrate were considerably decreased, and he just could not seem to shake the feeling of sadness and doom he had begun experiencing prior to his hospitalization. At a follow-up visit his cardiologist was concerned about the pastor's mood and symptoms and prescribed an antidepressant.

A forty-two-year-old former teacher had been appointed interim director of Christian formation at a medium-sized suburban parish seven months ago following the untimely death of the prior director in late summer. Since there was essentially no time to mount a regional search to replace the deceased director, the pastor offered the position to a loyal parishioner and mother of three who had been a volunteer catechist in the program for several years. The understanding was that this would be an interim appointment for one year which could become permanent.

Mrs. Simons was a bright, articulate, and politically correct individual who was actually quite insecure. She attempted to cover this insecurity with quick wittedness and wry humor. The pastor was quite taken by the hospitality she displayed in visits to her family and her sometimes off-beat humor. She never imagined herself as the director of an important parish program, but because the pastor told her he "had total confidence" in her, she reluctantly accepted the position. While Mrs. Simons quickly mobilized support among some of the catechists, students and parents, it was slow in coming from many others. Several were offended by her morbid and critical comments or jokes made in person or in the formation office's newsletter. It seemed that she cultivated a group of favorites whom she would bestow special benefits. Often she appeared to be clueless as to the direction the program should take. For a while she had asked for teacher and parent input on decisions, but since there was mounting dissension between her favorites and the rest of the parish community, this mode of decision-making was quickly abandoned. As time passed, the pastor became increasingly aware of the pessimistic outlook that underlay her humor and her actions and became convinced that an outside search for a permanent director was necessary.

Both ministers exhibit depressive features. In the first example, the minister meets DSM-IV criteria for depressive personality disorder, while in the second instance, the minister meets criteria for major depressive disorder. While there are some similarities, there are notable differences. This chapter will emphasize the dynamics of the depressive personality disorder as they are manifest in ministry personnel. However, to clarify the differences between the personality disorder and major depressive disorder a section will highlight these differences. In this chapter "depressive" minister refers to the depressive personality disorder.

## The Dynamics of the Depressive Personality Disorder

DSM-IV includes an investigational diagnosis called depressive personality disorder that has considerable face validity and clinical utility in understanding and treating a growing number of ministers today. Basic to this disorder of personality is a persistent and pervasive feeling of dejection, gloominess, joylessness, and unhappiness. Individuals with this disorder lack a sense of humor, are overly serious and seem to be incapable of relaxation and enjoyment. They view both the present and the future negatively. They judge others as harshly as they view themselves and tend to focus on others' failing rather than their positive attributes. They may exhibit a wry sense of humor or they may be openly cynical. In short, pervasive pessimism is a guiding factor in their lives.

Individuals with this personality style also tend to be quiet, passive, introverted. They tend to be followers rather than leaders and will often allow others to make a wide range of decisions for them. To the extent to which they have histories of early abusiveness, they tend to be ambivalent about authority figures. Though they may appear friendly and gregarious, they also fear isolation and being alone. They may experience periods of clinical depression and anxiety. Such episodes of depression are usually precipitated by a real loss or abandonment, such as divorce or the death of a spouse (Bornstein, 1993).

Depressive personality disorder has some similarities with dysthymic disorder. Dysthymic disorder is characterized as a chronic form of depression that lasts two years or longer, that has less severe depressive symptoms than major depressive disorders. While depressive personality disorder is a chronic disorder (actually, it is a life-long condition), it emphasizes cognitive (self-critical, negativistic, and pessimism), intrapersonal (unhappiness, brooding, inadequacy, and worthlessness), and interpersonal (judgmental and critical of others, and blaming) dimensions which dysthymic disorder does not.

Psychologically, individuals with dysthymic disorder grew up viewing themselves as victimized by life and doubting their capacities: "I'm hurt and inadequate." Their view of the world tends to be: "Things never work out for me, and I must rely on others to take care of me because I'm unable." Accordingly, their basic life strategy tends to be: "Don't get your hopes up, but rely on others at all costs." Because of these views, these individuals seldom develop effective skills in assertive communication, negotiation, and problem solving. As children, they were raised in families where parental criticism as well as overprotection were common. A likely parental injunction was: "You'll probably mess up by yourself, so you'll need our help." They were likely to have been both protected and criticized by adults as well as by siblings and peers. Not surprisingly, they expect similar care and protection as adults (Sperry, 1995).

## Two Types of Depressive Ministers

In his clinical study of ministry personnel, Weiser (1994) finds that the depressive personality, which he calls depressed/dependents, is common in ordained and lay ministry. He notes that individuals with depressive personalities, especially those with secondary narcissistic and compulsive features, are increasingly attracted to ministry positions today and are prime candidates for acceptance. He attributes this to recent changes in the culture and expectations of dioceses and religious congregations. This is reflected in screening guidelines which encourage and support dependence and compliance among candidates and screen out more independent and potentially rebellious candidates. Weiser contends that such screening guidelines inadvertently contribute to the increasing number of women being attracted to a variety of ministries, given that they are more likely to adopt and accept nurturing roles and characteristics than men.

These individuals tend to be dutiful, obedient, and loyal to superiors and institutions. That they tend to ascribe to traditional beliefs and values and orthodox practices is a given. They are more likely to be in renewal that occurs over a protracted period of time than in radical reform. Furthermore, they often have a history of volunteer activity, and tend to be cooperative rather than competitive.

According to Weiser, they do not see themselves on the cutting edge but rather as part of the larger and safer system that provides a sense of family, and feeling of belonging. Interestingly, they are likely to be viewed as healthy ministers, simply because they are not a threat to others. Often, they lack the healthy kind of drive expected of professionals, and so they are unlikely to be creative, visionary, or propose new ideas or new programs. Because they principally seek safety and caring from individuals and institutions, it should not be surprising that they are uncomfortable in prophetic and kingly/leadership roles.

Weiser describes two types of depressive ministers: higher functioning and lower functioning. The higher functioning type is described in the previous three paragraphs. The lower functioning depressive ministers are likely to meet criteria for depressive personality disorder. As such they are more distressed and impaired than their higher functioning counterparts. They are usually from severely dysfunctional families and have histories of physical, sexual, and emotional abuse. Family life was often punitive, abusive, and depressive. There was little bonding between parent and children. Not surprisingly, these ministers come to religious congregations and institutions searching for the nurture, safety, and love they did not receive as children. Much of the time these ministers are frustrated in this search since their needs are so exaggerated.

## The Spiritual and Religious Behavior of the Depressive Minister

In terms of religious behavior, these individuals appear to be orthodox in their beliefs and loyal followers, despite their ambivalence. This theme is reflected in their image of God, prayer life, and core issues in spiritual direction.

### Image of God

Depressive ministers tend to view God as all-powerful as well as merciless at times, and themselves as insignificant and not likely to experience his mercy. So, God is imaged as a blend of Rescuer and Punisher. When prayers are not "answered" or they are not otherwise "rescued," they are likely to fear that God has abandoned them.

### Prayer

Just as they depend on others to take care of them, they depend on God to take care of their needs. Not surprisingly, petitionary prayer predominates with these individuals: "God help me . . . protect me . . . take care of me . . . comfort me. . . ." When their prayers are not answered as they would like, they easily lose faith and fear being abandoned by God. At such times they turn to others for consolation and comfort.

*Reliance on Spiritual Direction and Pastoral Counseling*

Because of their sense of inadequacy and limited experience in taking responsibility for themselves, they tend to seek out religious counselors repeatedly. They may shift their dependency to spiritual directors or counselors and make numerous telephone calls to them for reassurance between interviews. If the counselor is away on a vacation, they may feel devastated by their sense of abandonment. Not surprisingly, they may have two or more counselors at once without telling them about each other. Interviews and telephone calls are ways of reducing anxiety about the fear of separation.

## Differences with Normal Depression and Major Depressive Disorder

This personality disorder differs from so-called normal depressive traits such as unhappiness, self-criticism, or guilt feelings. Rather than feeling 'blue' for a matter of hours or a day or so, individuals with the depressive personality disorder routinely experience these thoughts and feelings and also experience a significant degree of impairment in social or occupational functioning.

The personality disorder also contrasts with major depressive disorder—also called clinical depression—in a number of ways. The symptoms of major depression must be significantly distressing for at least two weeks—most of the day and nearly everyday—and usually affect intimacy as well as social and occupational functioning. Besides altered moods, clinical depression affects bodily functioning, activity level, and thinking. Changes in appetite, sleep, and activity are commonly noted. Clinically depressed individuals may have difficulty sleeping—sleeping too little or too much—decreased desire to eat or excessive eating. They may have very little energy, apathy or feel tired much of the time. Tearfulness is common. Interest in sex and pleasurable activities tends to be diminished. They may also experience impaired concentration, feelings of guilt, hopeless, and helplessness. Thinking may be slowed and confused. Suicidal thoughts during this period are not uncommon.

Sometimes ministers with this personality disorder can develop a concurrent major depressive disorder. Usually, this occurs following a significant loss and in the context of other life stressors. This combination of two types of depressive conditions is called "double depression." Treatment is usually more complicated than for major depressive disorder alone, usually requiring medication and/or hospitalizations.

## Interventions: Individual

The issue in the therapeutic treatment of this personality disorder is the persistent and pervasive pattern of pessimism and overdependency. Because of the centrality of the cognitive dimension of this disorder—pessimism, self-criticalness, and negativism—cognitively-oriented psychotherapy approaches have considerable promise. The focus of these cognitive approaches would be cognitive restructuring aimed at self-view and world-view. Medications, specifically the newer serotonergic blockers (such as Prozac, Zoloft, or Paxil) and sertonin-norepinehrine blockers (such as Serzone or Remeron), may be considered as adjunctives to psychotherapy.

Spiritual direction or spiritual counseling can be invaluable adjunctives to a cognitive-focused psychotherapy. The spiritual director might focus direction on the minister's distorted image of God and prayer style. A reasonable goal might be to expand the minister's image of God and supplement petitionary prayer with prayer of thanksgiving and gratitude. To the extent to which they have experienced abusiveness of all types during their upbringing, these ministers are unlikely to believe that they could ever be the "beloved" son or daughter "called by name." Spiritual direction could provide the context for such a spiritual and emotionally-corrective experience.

## Interventions: Organizational

### Screening

The matter of screening candidates for ministerial positions is not one to be taken lightly. While it is true that higher functioning individuals with depressive personality dynamics may appear to be ideal candidates because of their loyalty, obedience and cooperativeness, they are also individuals who cannot be expected to provide visionary and prophetic leadership in time of rapid social change. Certainly, lower functioning individuals—those who meet DSM-IV criteria for depressive personality disorder—are high-risk candidates. Whether in a training program or in actual ministry situations, they are quite difficult to work with. Since they want to please authority figures, they are seldom proactive and take few, if any, risks. Rather, their style is highly reactive and so they scan the environment looking for clues as to what those in authority desire. But even knowing that does not mean they can or will deliver. After all, they are ambivalent about authority figures. Not surprisingly, many experienced psychologists and psychiatrists who consult with religious organizations, including Conrad Weiser, Ph.D., insist that these candidates have no place in public ministries.

## Assignments

Religious administrators would do well to consider personality style when arranging ministry assignments. With regard to the depressive personality style, it should be noted that a pastoral or ministry team populated by more than one of these individuals will have difficulty being decisive and effective. There is a certain contagion effect—a depressive undercurrent that can pervade a group's functioning—that has been noted when no limits are set on this pessimism, black humor, or blame that emanates from this personality style.

## Culture of a Religious Organization

Sometimes, it can be observed that the culture of an entire province of a religious congregation or diocesan office reflects this depressive style. Since culture of an organization is greatly influenced by current leadership of an organization, it is likely that one or more of the provincial leadership team or diocesan officials exhibit this personality style or disorder. Such organizations are unlikely to effectively provide quality ministry service nor to recruit healthy candidates. Usually, outside professional consultation is necessary to effect a change in the organizational culture.

## References

Robert F. Bornstein, *The Dependent Personality*. New York: Guilford.

Len Sperry, *Handbook of Diagnosis and Treatment of the DSM-IV Personality Disorders*. New York: Brunner/Mazel, 1995.

Conrad Weiser, *Healers: Harmed and Harmful*. Minneapolis: Fortress Press, 1994.

# 9

## Passive-Aggressive Behavior in Ministry

During an interview early in his pontificate, Pope John XXIII was asked how many people worked in the Vatican. He paused, then smiled and said: "Oh, about half of them!" The implication was that there were many individuals who could be considered "deadwood" in various Vatican offices. Deadwood is a code word that refers to individuals who are not particularly productive nor effective in their jobs—meaning they are typically irresponsible and uncooperative—and may actually impair the efficacy of others around them. The psychological equivalent of deadwood is the term "passive-aggression." Passive-aggressive behavior and passive-aggressive personality style—which means an ongoing, consistent pattern of passive-aggressive behavior—is much more common among ministry personnel than it is among personnel in most other work settings.

The reason for this is quite simple: Most organizations are re-inventing themselves in order to maintain their basic viability in today's extremely competitive business climate. This has meant that once staid, bureaucratic organizations—both profit and non-profit—have been forced to undergo major structural changes and cultural transformation. These changes have effectively reduced or eliminated much passive-aggressivity in those organizations. Interestingly, this same trend has not appreciably impacted religious organizations and ministries, at least not yet.

Much has been written about passive-aggression as a diagnostic entity in clinical and corporate settings, but relatively little has been written about its impact in ministry settings. Accordingly, this chapter briefly describes passive-aggression and its manifestations in ministry settings, as well as ways of reducing its negative impact and effects.

Since psychiatric terminology continues to carry a stigma in both corporate and ministry circles, it may be more useful to frame passive-aggressive behavior and personality in organizational terms such as failure to listen, dysfunctional communication, decision-making difficulties, team work impasses, or conflict resolution problems. Effective organizational behavior, including that in ministry, is characterized by such indicators as active listening, assertive communication, collaborative decision-making, responsible leadership and effective team work, and conflict resolution based on problem-solving mode. In short, effective ministry is characterized by responsibility, cooperation, and commitment. The more responsibility, cooperation, and commitment characterizes a religious organization—whether parish, diocesan office or provincialate—the less likely these indicators will be evident.

One further caveat: Passive-aggression is best thought of as gradations of a theme from situation-specific, occasional expressions of passive-aggressive behavior to a generalized and constant expression of the passive-aggressive personality style disorder. It is only when passive-aggressivity becomes inflexible, maladaptive, and leads to significant impairment or distress that it constitutes the diagnostic entity of passive-aggressive personality disorder. The description of passive-aggressivity to follow reflects the more pathological gradations of this pattern.

## Dynamics of the Passive-Aggressive Personality

The predominant feature that characterizes the passive-aggressive personality is resistance to demands for performance both in occupational and interpersonal functioning. Passive-aggressive persons follow a strategy of negativism, defiance, and provocation, and are unable to make up their minds as to whether to adhere to the demands of others or to resist their demands. Consequently, their behavior is characterized by both passivity and aggressiveness. They appear to be ambivalent about nearly everything and cannot decide whether to be independent or dependent or whether to respond to situations actively or passively. They constantly struggle with the dilemma of whether to be submissive or assertive. They resolve this dilemma with a compromise: they express their anger and resistance indirectly through procrastination, dawdling, stubbornness, inefficiency, and forgetfulness. The passive-aggressive's resistance often reflects hostilities that they are afraid to show openly but instead have displaced on others. An aura of agreeableness and cordiality usually masks their negativistic resistance. They may smile when they "agree" to do something but under their breath they express their true thoughts and feelings.

The roots of passive-aggression are many. Biologically, the passive-aggressive is likely to have been dubbed a "difficult child." That is, their temperamental style during infancy would likely be characterized by emotional or affective instability. Psychologically, the passive-aggressive's view of themselves, of others, of the world, and of life's purpose is characterized by certain themes. They tend to view themselves as: "I am competent . . . well, not really competent" and other such contradictory appraisals. They tend to view life and other people as: "Life is a big bind. It's unfair, unpredictable, and unappreciative." As such the passive-aggressive person is likely to conclude: "So, it's safer to vacillate, temporize, oppose, and anticipate disappointment than to make and keep commitments."

Socially, the passive-aggressive person was most likely exposed to a parenting style noted by inconsistency. For example, as children they would sometimes experience severe and harsh discipline for a minor infraction, while on other occasions they received little or no discipline for the same infraction. Communication patterns were likewise inconsistent and contradictory. Because of this inconsistency they did not develop sufficient confidence and emotional stability to accurately assess what performance was expected of them.

Family schisms and sibling rivalry are common features of this pattern. These individuals were likely to have experienced being cut off and displaced from their parents' affection at the time of birth of a younger sibling, which contributed to their ambivalence of feelings and behavior. Often, these individuals were "chosen" to play a peacemaking role in conflicted families. Therefore, they became fearful of commitments, unsure of their own desires, competencies, the reactions of others, and afraid to express feelings directly. Indecisiveness, contradictory behavior, and fluctuating attitudes were practiced and reinforced. As children, and then as adults, they developed a pattern of shifting rapidly and erratically from one type of behavior to the next, while refusing to acknowledge their own responsibility for their difficulties. Therefore, their basic stance toward life is one of non-cooperation.

Because they firmly believe that life has not and cannot be fair, and that other persons have failed to cooperate with them, they feel justified in not only being uncooperative, but in making everyone else's life miserable. Because of their ambivalent self-image, they feel misunderstood, cheated, and unappreciated by life. Subsequently, they easily adopt the role of martyr or "injustice collector" to prove their distress and disaffiliation with others. Furthermore, they are convinced that nothing has ever or will ever work out for them. Needless to say, their selective memory screens out all the past successes they have experienced. Yet, they are resentful and envious of others. If things are going too well for themselves or others, they will make sure that they spoil it. By "snatching defeat out of the jaws of victory" they recreate their expected disillusionment.

Consequently, because of their temperament style and parenting pattern, which both formed and reinforced their perceptions about self and others, these individuals learn to appear agreeable, show good intentions, but not necessarily enact them. Over time, they establish a characteristic personality pattern marked by irresponsibility, uncooperativeness, and lack of commitment.

## Passive Aggression in Organizations

Given their negativism and subtle defiance, their ministry experience is often characterized by underachievement and dissatisfaction. While they may have initially presented themselves as talented and promising, they almost surely will disappoint the search committee that recommended them. In his studies of corporation in North America and in Europe, Manfred Kets de Vries, Ph.D. (1994), the noted psychoanalyst and organizational consultant, found that among all the personality styles, individuals with passive-aggressive personalities were extremely unlikely to occupy senior executive positions in for-profit corporations. It seems that profit and passive-aggressivity are basically incompatible. Interestingly, passive-aggressivity appears to be reasonably common among ministry personnel—whether in parishes, or diocesan or provincialate offices—at all levels, including top leadership positions.

Ministry settings seem to unwittingly foster passive-aggressivity by emphasizing external control, avoidance of conflict, and the suppression and denial of anger. Anger and resistance function like a cancer in such settings and can slowly destroy them. While passive-aggression may mimic commitment and cooperation, it is actually a counterfeit of commitment and cooperation. While these individuals may appear to be concerned and cooperative, they may actually subvert the organization's mission. They are ambivalent about commitments and often engage in negatively cooperative behavior, meaning that tasks don't ever seem to get completed, or their performances leave much to be desired. To the chagrin of their supervisors, passive-aggressive ministers tend to avoid self-discipline and sacrifice and appear to lack vision and focus in their ministries.

### Religious Behavior of Passive-Aggressive Ministers

How do passive-aggressive personalities function in religious settings? Basically, they give the impression of being committed and cooperative individuals, when in fact they are apt to sabotage or otherwise diminish the promise of ministry initiatives. They tend to be ambivalent about their ministry commitments and often engage in negative cooperation, meaning that what they agree to do never seems to get completed, or their performance leaves much to be desired.

They tend to hold harsh and unloving images of God, and their pessimistic spiritual outlook mirrors the rest of their rather unhappy, unproductive lives. Not surprisingly, obedience is not their strong suit, as they basically distrust and resent authority. Unfortunately, there is one "obedience" to which they are faithful: that is, not to appear angry or show negative affect. They are exasperating to other members of the community as well as to leaders, particularly because they are never at a loss to "excuse" their own shortcomings in their ministry or blame these shortcomings or failures on others.

Among the various personality types, the prayer life of passive-aggressive ministers is unique. While other personality types may storm heaven with all kinds of petitions or demands of God in their prayers, the passive-aggressive minister's prayer life is remarkable in that it hardly exists. While in public liturgical settings they may go through the motions of praying and may fool ministry peers, superiors, or parishioners, in private they may not even try. After all, they find it very difficult to trust God to meet their needs, so they don't even try.

Consistent with their overall pessimism, procrastination, and disorganization in their lives, these ministers tend to be so devoid of faith that their lives are not in any way meaningful in the present, and so devoid of hopefulness about anything working out for them in the future, that they seldom make efforts to grow spiritually. If they have begun spiritual direction, they are likely to be early drop-outs. If they start reading a religious inspirational book, they are unlikely to finish it. One might surmise that they would surely become atheists, but that requires more courage and resoluteness than they believe they are capable. So, instead of leaving the ministry they stay and make their lives and the lives of those around them miserable. Over time, these individuals have a reputation of being "spiritual sourpusses." In short, these individuals lead lives of quiet desperation; more specifically, lives of quiet spiritual desperation.

### Interventions with Passive-Aggressivity in Ministry Personnel

*Individual Interventions*

Many assume that long-term psychotherapy is the principal means of changing this pattern. Utilizing individual psychotherapy with the passive-aggressive personality-disordered minister can be a protracted and difficult process. Assuming that the individual sees the need for treatment and actually agrees to seek treatment, there is no guarantee of success. Stone (1993) notes that the passive-aggressive personality disorder is one of the few personality disorders that is considered non-amenable to treatment.

When individual psychotherapy is undertaken, the treatment strategy involves clarifying rules and expectations of treatment, challenging the minister's dysfunctional beliefs about self-worth, pessimism about life and people, hostile dependence on others, and oppositionalism. It also involves learning to exhibit an attitude of realistic optimism, acting more assertively and being reasonably cooperative. Treatment methods include insight or cognitive restructuring, paradoxical injunctions, and skill training in active listening, assertiveness, and interdependence. Such intensive individual psychotherapy can require two or more years. Many ministers drop out of such treatment prematurely, particularly if change threatens the balance of passive-aggressivity in the religious community or ministry team. This is ironical since the community or ministry superior typically urged this treatment in the first place! An alternative to long-term intensive individual psychotherapy is time-limited group therapy that focuses on teaching relational and coping skills as well as an understanding of the personality and organizational dynamics that trigger and reinforce passive-aggressivity.

## Organizational Interventions

When it becomes apparent that organizational dynamics trigger and reinforce passive-aggressive behavior, or passive-aggressive personality disorder for that matter, organizational interventions may be in order. It should be noted that organizations that have a passive-aggressive culture—and "supporting" organizational and leadership structures—will foster passive-aggressivity among its members. This means that such an organization or ministry will attract individuals with passive-aggressive personality styles. It will also powerfully reinforce specific passive-aggressive behaviors and attitudes among individuals who do not manifest the passive-aggressive personality style.

Accordingly, the goal of an organizational intervention is to change the organization's structures and culture that supports and fosters passive-aggressivity. Specifically, this includes policies, leadership practices, and organizational climate and norms which foster resistance, ambivalence, inconsistency, pessimism, chronic underachievement, and dissatisfaction. The goal is to fashion an organizational structure and culture that fosters and supports co-operation, commitment, consistency, hopefulness and pride, and achievement and job satisfaction. To achieve this goal the organizational interventions must focus on both individual changes as well as organizational changes.

When a "critical mass" of individuals in a particular ministry setting manifest the passive-aggressive personality style (or worse, the passive-aggressive personality disorder), it means these individuals are not likely to have learned the kind of coping and relational skills necessary for effective ministry. They may have deficits in one or more of these five skills: active listening, assertive communication, teamwork, decision-making, and problem-solving. Accordingly, the change process needs to intentionally focus on developing such skills among those individuals. Usually this can be accomplished in a group workshop setting facilitated by an outside consultant.

As far as modifying—or passive-aggression "proofing"—organizational structure, experience suggests that implementing a performance-appraisal or management system within the organization is essential. Typically, passive-aggressive organizations have never had such a system or the system is ineffective. Essentially, a performance appraisal system is a means by which a minister is held accountable for achieving specific results. If properly and effectively designed, the system identifies the minister's strengths and weaknesses, specifies the minister's level of performance relative to established performance standards and expectations, encourages self-development, provides recognition for accomplishments, and suggests areas for improvement.

The process of implementing a performance management system has great merit in that it requires all five of the above named skills become manifest. A major outcome of such a system is that it can significantly reduce passive-aggressivity. A related benefit is usually a noticeable increase in the organization's productivity and morale and often an increase in the minister's commitment to the ministry and cooperation with ministry peers.

An effective performance-appraisal system is a cooperative venture between a superior and a minister that begins with the establishment of specific performance standards for a given period of time, which is typically six months. The minister makes a written commitment to these standards and the superior agrees to help the minister toward achieving those standards by appropriate supervision, coaching, and encouragement. At the specified time, a performance-appraisal meeting is scheduled in which the minister's actual performance for the given time frame is measured against the previously written performance standards. Effective performance appraisals assume some level of proficiency with the skills of active listening, assertive communication, teamwork, decision-making, and problem-solving. Besides their value in the performance appraisal process, these skills are essential for effective overall organizational functioning.

Training groups of ministry personnel in active listening and assertive communication is widely available, so the focus of the remainder of this chapter will be on the other three skills. In its most generic sense, leadership can be thought of as a set of skills and a style of relating to others in terms of making decisions, managing people, and resolving conflicts.

Decision-making approaches span the continuum from the efficient, effective "decision-maker" to the erratic, procrastinating, buck-passing, foot-dragging "decision-avoider." The reality of life is that most decisions involve conflict, stress, and anxiety. "Decision-makers" accept these givens and proceed to collect information, weigh alternatives, and then make the best possible decision. "Decision-avoiders," on the other hand, often accumulate more information than they can possibly utilize, take a protracted period of time to consider alternatives, and effectively forestall the likelihood of reaching a decision. This delay may create a chain reaction that is costly to the rest of the organization. On the other hand, the decision-avoider may "pass the buck," so that someone else feels compelled to make that decision. Then, if the decision results in failure, it was the other person's fault.

The decision-avoider may frustrate others by foot-dragging, by not providing information needed by other members of the ministry team, or by making any number and type of excuses. Needless to say, the decision-avoiding stance is consistent with the passive-aggressive style. Thus, it is essential that the decision-making stance be expected of ministry personnel in leadership positions, and that through consultation, coaching or counseling that this skill be taught, facilitated, modeled, and reinforced.

A leader's style of managing others can be described in terms of a continuum where autocratic and democratic are the polar end-points. In organizational behavior language, it is common to characterize four points on this continuum as: tell, sell, consult, and join. "Tell" is the autocratic style of management that characterizes many religious organizations, while "sell" suggests that the leader attempts to influence others through persuasion without really listening to the concerns of others. In "consult" and in "join" it is not likely that the leader can truly engage in active listening. To adequately detect passive-aggressivity in ministry settings and attempt to deal with it constructively, the leader must possess the skill of active listening.

While it seems reasonable to expect that passive-aggressivity is most likely to be present in autocratically-lead organizations, it is not intuitively obvious that passive-aggressivity is also likely in extremely democratically-lead or "join" organizations. There is, in fact, a curvilinear relationship between an individual's freedom and passive-aggressivity. The more there is a "consultative" or cooperative relationship between leader and follower, the more likely that productivity, team work, morale, and acceptance of change will occur. However, it is not at all helpful to provide followers with more freedom than they are prepared to handle. The leader must monitor followers in such a way as to ensure that they are challenged but not overwhelmed. Passive-aggressive individuals find too much freedom as intolerable as too little freedom. In short, leaders must be able to really listen and hear.

The leader who has developed the ability to communicate skillfully is a blessing to any organization. Communication skills are among the most frequently sought in the training of leaders, since ineffectual communication is commonplace in organizational settings, including ministry settings. Not surprisingly, poor communication reinforces passive-aggressivity.

Candidates for leadership positions should be chosen for their capacity to communicate and to utilize a consultative style of leadership, particularly in organizations or ministry settings overly populated with passive-aggressive individuals. In addition to the skills of active listening and assertive communication, there are a few other prerequisites for effective leadership in ministry settings. These include a belief in the inherent growth potential of others, an attitude of trustworthiness, and the conviction that others will respond more favorably to encouragement than to punishment, neglect and inconsistency.

Finally, there are two approaches to conflict resolution: domination and problem-solving. Though both approaches have some merit, the problem-solving approach is more viable since it facilitates cooperation among individuals and encourages their respect for each other and their commitment to the organization. The problem-solving approach to conflict resolution encourages assertive self-expression while increasing organizational performance and effectiveness. On the other hand, domination and power-oriented approaches encourage the indirect expression of aggression among followers. Since frustration is increased, superiors may openly express aggression but similar expression of aggression is forbidden for others. Not surprisingly, conflict resolution by domination results in high turnover, particularly of committed, hard-working and psychologically healthy members of the organization. Of those who remain, some will continue in their characteristic passive-aggressive personality patterns, and others, who feel trapped in the organizational morass, may begin to exhibit more and more passive-aggressive behavior to cope with their frustrations. Like the other four skills, conflict resolution is a skill that can be learned in workshops and in work team settings.

## Concluding Note

Passive-aggressivity continues to be relatively common in ministry settings today. While passive-aggressive individuals are seldom promoted to top management positions in for-profit corporations, they can be found in senior leadership positions in religious institutions and ministry settings. The overall impact of this type of leadership has grave consequences for such institutions and ministries.

Effective and healthy ministerial functioning requires commitment and cooperation. Leaders and superiors in healthy ministry settings must hold up realistic expectations for productivity and satisfaction for their colleagues and place a premium on mutual communication, team work, and effective resolution of conflict. Any effort a superior makes to increase assertive communication and active listening in a ministry setting can and will reverse passive-aggressivity. Assertive communication contrasts with the indirect expression of anger, pessimism, and discouragement characteristic of passive-aggressive individuals. Likewise, active listening is incompatible with the relational style of passive-aggressive individuals. Similarly, if ministry leaders utilize a problem-solving approach to conflict resolution, approach decisions directly, and adopt a consultive style of leadership, they can expect cooperation and commitment rather than rebellion and passive-resistance from those who report to them.

While psychotherapy has only a limited place in changing this personality pattern, organizational interventions have considerably more promise. The importance of increasing five basic organizational-relational skills has been emphasized. Finally, the value of utilizing a performance-appraisal system and other accountability measures to positively influence productivity and morale and reduce passive-aggressivity has been advocated.

### References

Manfred Kets de Vries, *Prisoners of Leadership*. New York: Wiley, 1989.

Richard Parsons and Robert Wicks (eds.), *Passive-Aggressiveness: Theory and Practice*. New York: Brunner/Mazel, 1983.

Len Sperry, *Handbook of Diagnosis and Treatment of the DSM-IV Personality Disorders*. New York: Brunner/Mazel, 1995.

Michael Stone, *Abnormalities of Personality: Within and Beyond the Realm of Treatment*. New York: Norton, 1993.

# 10

# From Healing to Wholeness in Ministry

The Chinese character for change is composed of the symbols for crisis and opportunity. When it comes to the matter of impairment in ministry it seems incredulous that there could be any opportunity amid the anguishing crises that church leaders face today. Yet, truly effective leaders have the capacity for possibility thinking and visionary leadership in addition to the capacity for damage control and crisis management. Truly effective ministry leadership is prevention-oriented rather than simply crisis-oriented. It focuses on healing and wholeness.

This chapter focuses on prevention of ministry impairment. Prevention can be understood as a continuum consisting of three types of prevention: primary, secondary and tertiary. Tertiary prevention focuses on rehabilitation, i.e., efforts to contain or slow the progression of damage from a serious impairment. Psychotherapy and other psychiatric treatments with impaired ministers are forms of tertiary prevention. Secondary prevention involves identifying or treating a problem early enough to arrest or reverse early signs of ministry impairment. Primary prevention involves efforts to avoid ministry impairment before it occurs. Healing of ministers and communities takes place across this prevention continuum.

The leaders of a religious organization play a critical role in each of these three types of prevention. But, unquestionably, the most effective religious leaders are those who focus their efforts on the primary prevention of ministry impairment (Sperry, 1991).

Typically, religious leaders have dealt with ministry impairment by referring the impaired minister for psychiatric or substance abuse treatment—tertiary prevention. Granted the decision to initiate such a referral was necessary, it is seldom sufficient. Invariably, organizational dynamics are also involved. Therefore, policies, reward and sanction systems, and norms must be modified in order to reduce the likelihood of additional impairment—primary prevention. It may require a change in personnel—secondary prevention—such as removing a popular or highly visible minister from active service because he is no longer morally, spiritually, or psychologically fit for ministry (cf. Appendix: Fitness for Ministry: Indicators and Criteria). Needless to say, prevention efforts are unlikely to be successful unless the leadership of an organization fully supports and leads the change effort. Whatever the case, discernment, decisiveness, and courageousness are essential features of effective leadership that is visionary. In other words, prevention of ministry impairment requires visionary leadership.

This chapter briefly defines and delineates the concept of visionary leadership in ministry, along with its requisite skills and components. It describes and illustrates visionary leadership with reference to one particular type of ministry impairment: sexual misconduct involving ministry personnel.

## Visionary Leadership Defined

Today, the business and management literature is inundated with articles, chapters and books on leadership, particularly visionary leadership. Visionary leadership has been described as the action of the leader who takes charge, makes things happen, dreams, and then translates them into reality. The roles of direction setting, change agent, coach, and spokesperson define the job of the visionary leader (Nanus, 1992). Burt Director of the Leadership Institute at the University of Southern California provides a formula for successful visionary leadership: successful visionary leadership = shared purpose (vision (+) communication) (+) strategic thinking (+) appropriate organizational changes (+) empowered people.

So what does visionary leadership have to do with preventing ministry distress and impairment? Everything! Let me explain the

connection in terms of the current crisis involving sexual misconduct by clergy and religious, such as pedophilia which is an impairment, as well as a felony offense.

## Types of Responses to the Sexual Misconduct Crisis

There are at least four different types of responses that episcopal authorities can make to this crisis. The first type of response
basically involves denial: refusal to investigate, minimizing, ignoring, or blaming the victim. The second type of response involves
various reactive initiatives such as: setting up review commissions,
establishing policy statements, insuring treatment is offered
the victims, or advocating for the laicization of the perpetrators. The
third type involves proactive and/or preventive initiatives. The
guidelines for seminary training and celibacy and human sexual
development in the NCCB's document, *Program for Priestly Formation* (1982) and James Gill, M.D., S.J.,'s (1993) establishment
of the Christian Institute for the Study of Human Sexuality are examples of preventive and proactive initiatives. A fourth type of
response involves initiatives based on strategic planning and principles. Strategic planning is a process in which the leaders of an
organization or institution envision its future and develop the necessary goal and procedures for achieving that future. Strategically
managed organizations have clearly articulated and appropriated
vision or mission statements which galvanize members' commitment and guide their efforts in accomplishing the organization's
goals. By definition, strategically emerged organizations are visionary and proactive rather than crisis-oriented and reactive.

Organizations vary in their degree to which they are strategically managed and lead. In *Archbishop,* which is a detailed analy-
sis of the Catholic Church's power structure, Reese (1989) states
that episcopal governance is "primarily reactive and not proactive" and typically engages in crisis management. He observes
that while some archdioceses have developed mission statements
and pastoral plans, few do strategic planning, and most episcopal
decision making is incremental (short term, crisis-oriented) rather
than comprehensive (long term and future-oriented). Finally,
Reese notes that "where planning is taking place, it is usually in

response to a perceived crisis such as the decline in the number of priests."

What is the vision and mission of the American Catholic church? Do most of its members know and understand this mission statement? Are their thoughts, decisions, and behaviors guided by this mission? The answers are likely: unclear, no, and no. Herein, I believe, is the core problem. As the psalmist says: "Without a vision the people perish."

Some would agree that when society is relatively stable and unchanging, the missions of primary social institutions do not have to be explicitly stated because everyone knows what the church is about, what the family should be and what community government stands for. However, in times of rapid change and increased complexity and instability, institutional missions change and need to be clearly articulated. Reese argues that since Vatican II bishops have had to face a more complex and constantly changing environment, and lacking consensus on goals and lacking certainty on effectiveness, bishops have found themselves in the worst possible position to what has been traditionally considered "rational" decisions.

Reese contends that one reason episcopal leaders favor incremental planning over comprehensive and strategic planning is their lack of sophistication in the social sciences. I contend that political realities and economic necessity could reverse this view. Probably more than anytime in the recent past, the need for a proactive leader using visionary leadership skills has never been more evident.

But is visionary leadership compatible with Christian organizations? It could be argued that Jesus exemplifies the best of visionary leadership. The ministry of Paul clearly reflects a visionary leadership. The same could be said of many founders of religious Orders, as well as the first bishop of the U.S., John Carroll. The recent biography of Ignatius of Loyola implies that the founder of the Society of Jesus was a master of visionary leadership (Meissner, 1992).

## Visionary Leadership and the Prevention of Impairment

So how would visionary leadership deal with the sexual misconduct crisis? Basically, it wouldn't have permitted this situation to escalate into its present crisis proportions. Rather, visionary leadership would prevent crises from occurring.

Let's look at how visionary leadership could be applied to ministry to prevent further and future impairment based on Nanus' formula for successful visionary leadership.

## Shared Purpose

The first priority would be to clearly articulate the overall vision and mission of the American Catholic church and the specific roles of both clergy and religious in achieving this mission. The meaning of celibacy would also need to be articulated. These visions would need to be shared and discussed at the grass roots level to the point that commitment to the vision would be achieved.

## Appropriate Organizational Change

Next the Church's organization at its various levels would be examined for the purpose of reconfiguring structures, cultures and leadership style to support and insure that the mission would be accomplished (Sperry, 1990). Obviously, this would be a major undertaking and would start at points of greater need. Regarding sexual misconduct, several commentators note that the Church's culture of secrecy probably disposes and perpetuates sexual misconduct. Sipe (1990) suggests that "there is no other single element so destructive to sexual responsibility among clergy as the system of secrecy that has both shielded behavior and reinforced denial." He describes this culture or system of secrecy as "partially in the service of confidentiality necessary for the individual's growth, but it is also in the service of not giving scandal, thus sealing institutionally the system into a mode of operation that perpetuates the very problem it is designed to eradicate." Furthermore, this system defines "any sexual problem" as "acts" isolated from its developmental and relationship implications . . . equating incidents with sin. The sin is submitted to the system of secrecy . . . It is then "forgiven" or "forgotten" with minimal awareness of the relationship of the behavior to the person and his responsibilities. Visionary leadership would modify the institutional culture accordingly and quickly. Furthermore, the crisis management style of episcopal leadership and their emphasis on short-term incremental planning would be replaced with long-range strategic planning.

## Strategic Thinking

Essentially, strategic thinking is a way of conceptualizing problems and their solution as well as considering all decisions in light of an organization's mission and goals. Strategic thinking reduces vague and muddled thinking and wishes. When episcopal leaders and ministry personnel practice strategic thinking, they would likely consider how Jesus might act and respond in a given situation. When the matter of sexual misconduct is considered, seminary and formation personnel would discuss ways of implementing guidelines on training candidates about celibacy (i.e., NCCB's The Program of Priestly Formation or Gill's Christian Institute for the Study of Human Sexuality, etc.).

## Empowered People

Finally, when: "people buy into the vision, they possess the authority, that is, they are empowered to take actions that advance the vision, knowing that such actions will be highly valued by all those who share the dream" (Nanus, 1992). Empowerment is frequently discussed among ministry personnel, but less often demonstrated, probably because episcopal leaders are not convinced of its values or are afraid of its impact. Nevertheless, visionary leaders empower individuals and these individuals then respond with effective, responsible behavior. Regarding sexual misconduct: when Catholic ministers and the people they work with are empowered to form their consciences and are expected to act respectfully and responsibly, sexual exploitation would be reduced or eliminated.

Does application of the visionary leadership formula and principles seem unrealistic and unlikely to be achieved in the American church? If it was possible how long would it take? In organizations, including religious organizations, the usual time span for transitioning from a traditional mode of operation to a visionary mode of operations is 2.5–5 years, even among large multinational corporations. It might take that amount of time for a given diocese or province to change, too.

## Concluding Note

Preventing ministry impairment requires the support and active involvement of religious leaders in all three types of prevention, but particularly primary prevention. Truly effective leadership is not afraid to consider that not only are impaired ministers in their organization, but that their very organization may be impaired and impairing some of its members by its policies, culture, and norms.

Ministry leadership has a choice: to continue in its crisis management mode or not. No single policy change, program or institute or sexuality training program—no matter how proactive—can in and of itself change individual behavior in an institution which significantly impacts how and what that person thinks, feels, and acts. Perhaps another way of framing all this is to say that impaired religious institutions largely shape the impaired behavior of its ministers. To really change or prevent impairment requires that both individual and institution change.

## References

James Gill (1993), "Better Formation for Celibacy Needed," *Human Development* 14, 1, 3–4.

William Meissner (1992), *Ignatius of Loyola: The Psychology of a Saint.* New Haven: Yale University Press.

Burt Nanus (1992), *Visionary Leadership*. San Francisco: Jossey-Bass.

National Conference of Catholic Bishops (1982), *The Program of Priestly Formation, 3rd ed.* Washington, D.C.: United States Catholic Conference.

Thomas Reese (1989), *Archbishop: Inside the Power Structure of the American Catholic Church.* San Francisco: Harper and Row.

Richard Sipe (1990), *A Secret World: Sexuality and the Search for Celibacy.* New York: Brunner/Mazel.

Len Sperry (1990), "Blind Leadership in Stumbling Organizations," *Human Development* 11, 4, 24–29.

Len Sperry (1991), "Determinants of a Minister's Well-Being," *Human Development* 12, 2, 21–26.

# Appendix

## Fitness for Ministry: Indicators and Criteria**

Religious superiors, diocesan officials, and pastors are charged with the difficult task of determining when a given individual is or is not fit for active ministry. The decision may be rather straight-forward as in certain instances, such as conviction for pedophilia. But the decision may be quite complex and difficult, especially when ministry unfitness is confused with ministry impairment. What criteria should be used to determine fitness/unfitness?

### Three Ministry Examples

The first case involves an associate pastor who was arrested for driving under the influence of alcohol. A short account of the incident appeared in the daily newspaper. A week prior to the arrest the rectory housekeeper observed what she described as slurred speech. While in an alcohol detoxification program it is determined that he was clinically depressed—secondary to the death of his younger brother—and was prescribed antidepressant treatment. No prior history of substance abuse nor serious ministry problems were found. After a four-week hospitalization, he is discharged.

The second case involves a lay music minister in a large urban parish with a reputation for being colorful and off-beat. While en-dearing for some, this dramatic flair had been upsetting for others who contend that eucharistic liturgies were essentially musical performances rather than occasions of worship. He downplayed allegations of liaisons with married female parishioners. Complaints of being self-absorbed, demanding, indifferent to others' needs, and non-compliance with the pastor's directives and limit-settings were also noted. Nevertheless, the pastor enjoyed the type of liturgical music played and was reluctant to support the parish council's plan to not renew the minister's contract.

The third case involves a nun who is diocesan coordinator of RCIA programs. Although possessing excellent credentials, her performance had not matched her promise. She was absent or late for appointments, inconsistent in the supervision of her staff, and had failed to respond to her boss's coaching on handling staff matters. She reportedly loses her temper and cries following the least of interpersonal slights. At a recent budget meeting she raised eyebrows when she screamed out that if the bishop and chancellor really cared about her or RCIA candidates, they would not cut her budget. Her personal life is reported to be chaotic, and her associates wonder if the scars on her wrists represent suicide gestures.

On first glance, it might seem that the priest with the newspaper-reported drinking problem and arrest would be unfit for ministry, while the music minister and RCIA coordinator, although troublesome, are probably fit for ministry if not in their present jobs, at least in some other. Those who indicated that the priest was unfit probably based their determination on a criterion such as public scandal. There are problems with the use of a single criterion as scandal. For instance, a priest's intoxication may not as much as raise eyebrows in one community, while it may ignite a firestorm in another. Furthermore, what constitutes scandal for a child is likely to be different for an adult. For this reason, additional criteria can be useful in determining whether an individual is fit or not for engaging in active ministry.

## Moral, Spiritual, and Psychological Ideals in Ministry

The proposed criteria reflect basic moral, spiritual, and psychological ideals deemed essential to Christian ministry. These ideals include honesty, integrity, self-surrender, and transparency of character. It is presumed that the more the minister strives after these ideals, the more likely the minister will function as a credible and effective witness of the Gospel, and vice versa. Thus, a ministry based on honesty and integrity is preferable to one based on dishonesty, misrepresentation, pretense, and lack of integrity. Furthermore, a ministry centered on the Lord and characterized by self-surrender and generosity is preferable to one that is based on self-aggrandizement and self-serving actions.

Similarly, a minister who strives to be transparent and genuine in dealings with others is preferable to a minister who is gamy or opaque. There are no surprises with transparent ministers: they are who they represent themselves to be. On the other hand, there are surprises with ministers with opaque characters, as they often lead double lives. For instance, in time it comes to light that the associate pastor or music minister who has been so enthusiastic with the youth ministry is actually a sex offender.

Corresponding to these moral and spiritual ideals are certain psychological features. The more ministers strive toward these moral and spiritual ideals, the more likely they are to be helpful and collaborative, to be forgiving and conciliatory, and to be empathic and compassionate. Furthermore, they are less likely to be self-absorbed and self-serving, to demand to be the center of attention, to control and manipulate others, to seek revenge, and to be indifferent to the needs of others.

In short, individuals fit for ministry strive for the Christian ideals of transparency, integrity, honesty, self-surrender and compassion, over opaqueness of character, lack of integrity, dishonesty, and self-serving actions. Table 1 summarizes these themes.

| FIT FOR MINISTRY | UNFIT FOR MINISTRY |
|---|---|
| 1. Honesty | 1. Dishonesty |
| 2. Integrity | 2. Lack of Integrity |
| 3. Self-surrender | 3. Self-serving actions |
| 4. Transparency of character | 4. Opaqueness of character |

*Table 1: Moral Indicators of Fitness/unfitness For Ministry*

For the most part, the severe personality disorders, particularly the reactive or malignant narcissistic personality disorder, reflects the "unfit for ministry" indicators, and their corresponding psychological features.

## Criteria for Ministry Fitness/unfitness

The following criteria can be useful in discerning whether an individual is fit or not for engaging in active ministry. While these criteria involve observable maladaptive behavior and are psychologically-based, they also reflect the basic moral and spiritual ideal of honesty, integrity, and compassion in ministry. Six criteria can be specified, with the first being the basic criterion and the others being supportive criteria:

1. A consistent pattern of opaqueness of character, lack of integrity, dishonesty, and self-serving action. Such a pattern usually characterizes a severe personality disorder, particularly the narcissistic, antisocial, borderline, or paranoid personality disorders. The presence of such psychiatric disorders as major depressive disorder, bipolar disorder (manic-depression) or panic disorder in the *absence* of one of these severe personality disorders would not necessarily indicate unfitness for ministry. On the other hand, psychiatric disorders which severely limit the individual's ability to remain in contact with reality or relate to others such as schizophrenia, delusional disorder, dissociative disorder, severe obsessive-compulsive disorder, or a chronic incapacitating substance dependence disorder might render that individual unfit for active ministry.

2. Unwillingness to participate or unresponsiveness to coaching, spiritual direction, or other limit-setting efforts to change or ameliorate the maladaptive pattern.

3. Refusal to comply with a referral for psychiatric treatment (inpatient, residential, medication evaluation, or individual or group therapy) or failure to meet treatment goals and improve sufficiently.

4. Criminal behavior, whether or not it results in criminal charges and conviction, or severe problems with authority, i.e., continued defiance or rule-breaking.

5. Presence of a substance addiction, relationship addiction, or behavioral addiction (i.e., gambling).

6. Significant concern about the impact of the individual minister's behavior, or a career history marked by inconsistency or poor performance in ministerial duties which impacts the spiritual and psychological well-being of those being ministered. Examples are spreading harmful rumors, physical, verbal or emotional abusiveness, being chronically late or absent from assignments, or being the source of scandal.

Generally speaking, the first criterion plus one or more of the supporting criteria are strongly suggestive of unfitness for ministry. Two exceptions are noted: (1) if the individual does not meet all the DSM-IV diagnostic criteria for a severe personality disorder, then three or more of the supportive criteria of unfitness should be present; and (2) a single criterion, such as admission of guilt and conviction of a felony offense such as homicide or pedophilia, is probably indicative of unfitness. On the other hand, arrest and conviction for driving under the influence of alcohol without the presence of a severe personality disorder or another of the above criteria would not necessarily qualify for unfitness. Figure 3 summarizes these criteria.

## Ministry Impairment Compared to Unfitness for Ministry

A basic psychological tenet is that personality and character are stable and relatively impervious to change. Unfortunately, this means that the prognosis for most, if not all, individuals who are determined to be unfit for ministry by the above criteria is very guarded. Unfitness must be distinguished from impairment since there is some overlap between the two.

Generally speaking, impairment involves a serious medical or psychiatric condition that greatly reduces or prevents individuals from performing most or all of their ministerial functions. On the

---

### FITNESS FOR MINISTRY CRITERIA

The following criteria can be useful in discerning whether an individual is fit or not for engaging in active ministry. While these criteria involve observable maladaptive behavior and are psychologically-based, they also reflect the basic moral and spiritual ideals of honesty, integrity, and compassion in ministry. Six criteria can be specified, with the first being the basic criterion and the others being supportive criteria:

1. A consistent pattern of opaqueness of character, lack of integrity, dishonesty, and self-serving action. Such a pattern usually characterizes a severe personality disorder, particularly the narcissistic, antisocial, borderline, or paranoid personality disorders. The presence of a concomitant psychiatric disorder, such as major depressive disorder or obsessive-compulsive disorder in the *absence* of one of these severe personality disorders would not necessarily indicate unfitness for ministry.

2. Unwillingness to participate or unresponsiveness to coaching, spiritual direction or other limit-setting effort to change or ameliorate the maladaptive pattern.

3. Refusal to comply with a referral for psychiatric treatment (inpatient, residential, medication evaluation, or individual or group therapy) or failure to meet treatment goals and improve sufficiently.

4. Criminal behavior, whether or not it results in criminal charges and conviction, or severe problems with authority, i.e., continued defiance or rule-breaking.

5. Presence of a substance addiction, relationship addiction, or behavioral addiction (i.e., gambling).

6. Significant concern about the impact of the individual minister's behavior, or a career history marked by inconsistency or poor performance in ministerial duties which impacts the spiritual and psychological well-being of those being ministered. Examples are spreading harmful rumors, physical, verbal or emotional abusiveness, being chronically late or absent from assignments, or being the source of scandal.

Generally speaking, the first criterion plus one or more of the supporting criteria are strongly suggestive of unfitness for ministry. Two exceptions are noted: (1) if the individual does not meet all the DSM-IV diagnostic criteria for a severe personality disorder, then three or more of the supportive criteria of unfitness should be present; and (2) a single criterion, such as admission of guilt and conviction of a felony offense such as homicide or pedophilia, is probably indicative of unfitness. On the other hand, arrest and conviction for driving under the influence of alcohol without the presence of a severe personality disorder or another of the above criteria would not necessarily qualify for unfitness.

---

*Figure 3: Criteria for Ministry Fitness/Unfitness*

other hand, individuals judged unfit to minister can often perform aspects of their ministry functions sufficiently well enough to avoid early detection. Impairments are potentially treatable and may be curable. For instance, many common psychiatric disorders such as depression, bipolar disorder, anxiety disorders, and even alcohol abuse, are very amenable to psychiatric treatment and have fair to good prognoses. This contrasts with the severe personality disorders which are much less amenable to treatment and thus have poor prognoses. Personality disorders may be present in some, but not all, impaired ministers. However, severe personality disorders are almost always present in unfit ministers. Accordingly, the prognosis for those individuals adjudged unfit for ministry is very guarded or poor. Unfortunately, this effectively limits options for unfit ministers. Thus, in order to reduce chaos or unrest in a religious community, parish, or diocesan office, as well as reduce legal liability, many, if not most of these individuals, are removed from active ministry. Furthermore, it is conceivable, though rare, that a minister can be both impaired and unfit for ministry.

## Ministry Examples Revisited

Returning to the cases, it should now be apparent that the priest arrested for driving under the influence would not meet the criteria for ministry unfitness. Although there is evidence of Axis I disorders—major depression and alcohol abuse—there is no indication of a severe Axis II personality disorder, nor refusal to comply with treatment or limit setting, nor obvious scandal—only the housekeeper had witnessed the slurred speech on a single occasion. Since no mention was made of failure to function ministerially, it is also unlikely that impairment is present.

While it may appear that the other two cases are less serious, reviewing them in light of the proposed criteria suggest that they are much more serious. In fact, both meet criteria for ministry unfitness. The music minister meets four of the six criteria. A narcissistic personality disorder with antisocial or psychopathic features is present in the music minister. Chapter 2 describes the reactive or malignant narcissistic personality exemplified by this minister. His defiance of the pastor's authority, unresponsiveness to the pastor's limit setting, and significant concerns about the impact of his behavior on parishioners, i.e., liaisons with women, as well as empathic deficits suggest his unfitness for this and probably any other active ministry. Similarly, the nun meets three of the six criteria. She would meet criteria for borderline personality disorder, one of the most severe and difficult to treat Axis II disorders. Additional criteria include unresponsiveness to coaching provided by her boss, and significant inconsistency in her job performance.

**Grateful acknowledgment to the Most Reverend Richard J. Sklba, auxiliary bishop of the Archdiocese of Milwaukee for his thoughtful review of these criteria and his suggestion of "opaqueness of character, dishonesty, lack of integrity, and self-serving" as moral indicators of unfitness for ministry. Bishop Sklba's indicators deftly bridge the psychological and moral domains, and are a seminal contribution to the ongoing discussion of the determinants of fitness for ministry.

## References

Robert McAllister, *Living the Vows: The Emotional Conflicts of Celibate Religious*. Harper & Row, 1986.

Len Sperry, *Handbook of Diagnosis and Treatment of DSM-IV Personality Disorders*. Brunner/Mazel, 1995.

Len Sperry, "Preventing Impairment in Ministers" *Human Development* 14, 2, Summer, 1993.

# Index